CINEMATOGRAPH OF WORDS

WRITING SCIENCE

EDITORS Timothy Lenoir and Hans Ulrich Gumbrecht

CINEMATOGRAPH OF WORDS

Literature, Technique, and Modernization in Brazil

Flora Süssekind

TRANSLATED BY Paulo Henriques Britto

STANFORD UNIVERSITY PRESS

STANFORD, CALIFORNIA 1997

Stanford University Press
Stanford, California
© 1997 by the Board of Trustees of the
Leland Stanford Junior University
Printed in the United States of America

Originally published in Portuguese in 1987 as
*Cinematógrafo de letras: Literatura, técnica e
modernização no Brasil* (São Paulo: Companhia
das Letras), © Flora Süssekind

CIP data are at the end of the book

For Mário Sérgio

Acknowledgments

This text was written when the Philology Department of the Research Division of Fundação Casa de Rui Barbosa, where I work, was preparing new editions of some "premodernist" novels that, although now largely forgotten, are relevant to the study of Brazilian intellectual production during the period from the 1880's to the 1920's. My work in selecting some of these volumes suggested this attempt to reinterpret the period, focusing particularly on the close relationship between literature and technique that characterized it.

I would like to thank my fellow researchers in the Philology Department for their support and their interest in my work. Once again, my thanks to Rachel T. Valença for reading the draft; to Aluísio Azevedo Sobrinho and Plínio Doyle for access to their private collections and some bibliographical suggestions; to Júlio Castañon Guimarães and Homero Senna for lending me books and giving me invaluable information; and to Nádia Seckler for her patient typing. I would also like to thank Francisco Foot Hardman for his precise and honest criticism of another essay of mine and for lending me his unpublished dissertation on the building of the Madeira-Mamoré railroad, which helped me to reflect on some of the unfortunate ambiguities that characterized Brazil's process of modernization at the turn of the century.

I am grateful to the Fundação Casa de Rui Barbosa for allowing me access to its library, special collections, and photo archives, and for providing reproductions of the figures that appear here.

F.S.

Contents

A Note to the Reader

In quotations, spaced ellipsis points (. . .) indicate Flora Süssekind's omissions of portions of the original text; closed suspension points (...) replicate ellipses in the original.

CINEMATOGRAPH OF WORDS

CHAPTER 1

In Place of an Epigraph

Right at the outset, I run into a difficulty: how to make an epigraph out of moving images? Perhaps a series of movie stills would do the job. But this would not convey the exact duration of each shot. There would be no sound, no dreamlike sense—so characteristic of the movies—of appearing on the screen and then vanishing without a trace, which would be utterly lost in a sequence of fixed pictures on a page. Thus the very notion of converting a moving image into a typographical image—the idea of a cinematograph of words—seems nearly paradoxical.

Nevertheless, a series of movie sequences haunt these pages and provide it with an epigraph of sorts. Sometimes only the sound is relevant; at other times, it is a close-up that matters, the close-up of an object: a typewriter. The movie is Wim Wenders's *Hammett* (1982); the images in question are not contained in a single sequence or scene. I have in mind a number of hints that convey the feeling that the most powerful image in the movie is not the city of San Francisco, or former Pinkerton gumshoe Jimmy, or the missing Crystal Ling—not even Dashiel Hammett himself. The image that fills the entire screen, that is repeatedly shown in the foreground, sometimes superimposed upon others, is Hammett's typewriter. In the final sequence, in a deliberate cliché, it is this typewriter that types on the film itself, as if upon a page, the words "THE END," with which the movie is over.

In fact, the film begins with a superimposition of sounds. The noises and sights of a city street, which place the story in San Francisco, are gradually overlaid with the insistent patter of a typewriter. Then the camera shows a man, his back to the window, typing away; a pile of blank and typed sheets; a black iron typewriter; and finally the keyboard. It is as if these were the central elements in the story, this other story that, together with the rhythmic sound of the typewriter, seems to be superimposed on the intricate criminal plot: the story of a professional writer who writes directly on his typewriter, who has no time to draft outlines by hand, who writes books to be published immediately in cheap paperback editions, with loud, eye-catching covers. It seems, then, that for this professional writer and detective the typewriter is an inseparable companion; we see it in extreme close-ups that, accompanied by the mechanical sound of typing, show no more than the round keys, the fast-spinning spool, a succession of types, as if the words were being typed not on paper but on the screen itself—celluloid letters.

This representation of a machine seems to hint at other stories—stories of other intellectuals whose work closely depends on technique, including the professionals of the movie industry. It seems only natural that Wim Wenders, while having problems with his producer Francis Ford Coppola and at the same time shooting another movie (*The State of Things*) about the process of producing a movie, should have made the typewriter the central image in *Hammett*. It functions as a sort of additional clue, suggesting that one cannot understand the life of this author of novels and detective stories—or the work of a filmmaker—without taking into account the impositions of professionalization, the pressures of producing at an industrial pace, and the traces left by technical resources.

Hammett, with its images of love and its phantasmagoria of machines: this, then, is the epigraph of this attempt to analyze the relations between literature and technique in Brazil from the 1880's to the 1920's. For it is in these relations that we can perhaps see more clearly the shape of this period, usually defined from a literary perspective as "pre-" or "post-" something or other, only rarely seen in terms of its own characteristics. One such characteristic is the intense interaction with the new technological perspectives then arising in Brazil, the beginning of the professionalization of writers, and a revision of the concept of literature, redefined as technique.

This essay inevitably responds to three recent surveys of "premodernism," all published in 1983, each of which adopted a different analytic viewpoint—none of them similar to the one I will follow. Paes (1983) relies on a characteristic symbolist resource—correspondences—to reexamine the premodernist period in terms of a number of analogous aesthetic procedures that range freely from the field of visual art to that of literature. Taking into consideration the flowery, ornamental language of the period, as well as art nouveau drawing and arts and crafts, Paes proposes the concept of art nouveau literature, to cover both the worldly journalism of João do Rio (the pen name of Paulo Barreto) and Théo Filho and the regionalist universe of Valdomiro Silveira and Afonso Arinos, as well as the "surface" ornamentation of Coelho Neto and the pompous scientific vocabulary of Euclides da Cunha, which he characterizes as ornamentalism that is "consubstantial" with the situations the author describes.[1] These, then, are José Paulo Paes's major points: the correspondences between visual and verbal art, and the art nouveau label to designate cultural production at the turn of the century.

Sevcenko (1983) bases his analysis on the differentiation between groups of intellectuals in the period—the "winners" (Coelho Neto, Olegário Mariano, etc.), "fashionable authors," "who merge with the social and political *arrivistes*" (pp. 103–4); the "resigned" and excluded (which, according to Sevcenko, included "particularly the symbolists, decadents, and late-Romantic holdovers" (p. 105); and the "missionaries," characterized by "alienation"—not at all resigned, but rather "compulsory"—from public life, accompanied by a "passionate sociopolitical commitment" (p. 119); here the most outstanding examples are Lima Barreto and Euclides da Cunha. On the basis of this intellectual typology, Sevcenko analyzes Brazilian intellectual production during the First Republic. Thus the boundaries of his reading are set a priori by a periodization drawn from political history; and from a single viewpoint—the borders and groups established in the intellectual world—the literature of the period is observed, serving at the same time as illustration and frame of reference for this viewpoint.

Finally, Hardman (1983) presents an analysis of Brazilian cultural production between the 1890's and 1922. His work's central concern is to detect how this transition to "modernity" took place. Discarding dualistic interpretations of modernism—which tend to see its "innovative aspects" as "imports from the European avant-gardes" and its "backward aspects" as resulting from "domestic determinations"[2] (p. 114)—Hardman investigates how it was possible to "integrate this 'foreign' aspect into the domestic process of intellectual and artistic elaboration, precipitating the crisis of discourse and intervening internally in its solutions" (p. 115).

To answer this question, Hardman analyzes the libertarian social literature of Avelino Fóscolo, Curvelo de Mendonça, Cornélio Pires, Rocha Pombo, Fábio Luz, Elísio de Carvalho, and Martins Fontes, as well as the proletarian newspapers of the early twentieth century and the "growing presence of an international labor force" (p. 116) in the major Brazilian cities. And, he believes, the existence of a growing industrial proletariat largely made up of immigrants had a decisive impact on the rise of a climate favorable to modernism. "The modernist cosmopolitanism was not made possible . . . by 'foreign dependence,'" Hardman argues, "but rather by the cracks in the prevailing order that the presence of a numerous, if anonymous, international labor force had been causing for at least three decades" (p. 116). Thus Hardman's major concern is the transition, the path leading to modernity; and his object of analysis is a specific part of early-twentieth-century cultural production: libertarian literature, proletarian newspapers, and anarchist theater.

Here, however, I adopt a different approach. My concern is to determine what is *distinctive* about the literary production of the period. Rather than focus on its relations with visual art, with a rising social class, or with a sociopolitical division within the educated classes of Brazilian society, I examine the *crônica*,[3] poetry, and fiction of these three decades in terms of the encounter with a burgeoning technological and industrial landscape, an encounter that began warily and hesitantly and later turned into flirtation, friction, or appropriation.

I examine this encounter from two angles. The first is explicit representation: the portrayal in literature of modern artifacts, new means of transportation and communication, the newborn industries of advertising and commercial publication in early-twentieth-century Brazil. After these explicit marks have been duly analyzed, we shall see how these close contacts with the technological world came to shape cultural production—that is, not how literature *represents* technique, but how literary technique changed as it incorporated procedures characteristic of photography, film, and poster art. Its transformation was consistent with the significant changes taking place in the perceptions and sensibilities of the population of the major Brazilian cities of the time, attuned to the domination of the image, the instant, and technology as all-powerful mediators of the experience of the urban landscape, time, and a subjectivity constantly under the threat of extinction.

And though I have used the typewriter (and Brazilian writers and their reactions to it) as the emblem of the changes suffered by literary technique from the 1880's to the 1920's, the starting point of my analysis is another artifact: a misplaced gramophone.

CHAPTER 2

The Hand and the Machine

Let us begin with *Vida ociosa*, a novel by Godofredo Rangel originally published in installments in *Estadinho* (the afternoon edition of the daily *O Estado de S. Paulo*) and the magazine *Revista do Brasil* in 1917. Toward the end of the book, there is a scene that provides an accurate illustration of one effect of the technical innovations—disseminated throughout the country at an ever-increasing pace since the later decades of the nineteenth century—on the everyday lives and the changing sensibilities of the most active producers of culture in Brazil at the turn of the century and in the early decades of the twentieth century, an influence that had a decisive impact—by contrast, imitation, or stylization—on their literary technique. In this particular scene (as, indeed, throughout the novel), the dialogue between literary form and modern artifacts takes place through displacement and contrast—contrast bordering on irony. This is clearly seen when Félix, the narrator, turns suddenly from the many legal documents he is supposed to be studying to examine a gramophone:

It was a precious old machine that had been lent to a succession of users and had eventually become sadly ungovernable. But after the last time it was lent, it returned with rare virtues that were most pleasing to me: even without a record, it played Wagnerian music—loud, stormy music. I switched it on and it began. First there was a dull rumble, as of a storm brewing; suddenly peals of thunder rolled, interspersed with inexpressible squeals. Then it subsided and began to chirp and creak with such animal tones that it stirred the very fibers of one's heart. (Rangel n.d.: 131)

This description seems to subvert the usual functioning of the machine. What is praised in the gramophone is not its ability to mechanically reproduce previously recorded sounds, but the fact that, being out of order, the machine seems to be closer to nature, producing sounds that are reminiscent of thunder and animal cries. What impresses the narrator is not the machine's technical performance but what lies beyond the reach of technology. It is because it has become useless that the gramophone acquires meaning in a world ruled by emotion, the world of *Vida ociosa*. Here one of the most popular technological innovations is represented, but in such a way as to neutralize its importance among the multitude of episodes, digressions, and memories that are displayed, in slow succession, throughout the novel.

Nevertheless, the fact remains that it was necessary at one point to mention a machine—a broken gramophone. This was done in part to heighten the machine's aura by making it dysfunctional, in part because it was inevitable that the novel should mention some component of the modern façade then being imposed on the country, even in as unlikely a context as the rural setting of Rangel's novel. It is as if the technological innovations forced themselves upon the writer. This sometimes perplexing, sometimes perverse fact seems to draw attention to a characteristic trait of Brazilian fiction from the 1890's to the 1920's: the dialogue between literary form and technical images, sound recording, mechanical movement, and new printing processes. This dialogue between literature and the media, in its various versions, is perhaps distinctive of Brazilian literature of the period in a much more substantial way than the many labels usually attached to it, whether beginning with neo- (Parnassianism, regionalism, classicism, Romanticism), with post- (naturalism), or with pre- (modernism).

The versions of this dialogue are indeed various: though in Rangel technology is represented as an old gramophone—perversely as out of place as the many "dead objects" in the nostalgic stories in Afonso Arinos's *Pelo sertão* (1898), for instance—this is by no means the most common way in which modern machinery is represented in the Brazilian literature of the period. João do Rio's texts, for instance, were always on cozy terms with the new media of reproduction, printing, and distribution; the author not only presents them in a favorable light but also shows their influence on his literary technique. One of the most evident examples of this influence is a reference, in *A profissão de Jacques Pedreira* (1911), to a biograph show during a charity party:

The tents, in fact, were very well arranged along the aisles; flower and card tents lay in ambush; those selling sweets and drinks were quite visible. Theatrical sketches were performed on the dais near the bar, whose owner had promised, at the last moment, to turn on the biograph during the evening's intervals—for free. Those ladies found a way of having everything for free. Even the biograph. (Rio 1911: 48)

"Even the biograph": the narrator seems to value highly this early version of the cinematograph. Another example, also by João do Rio, comes from a 1910 text, "O dia de um homem em 1920" (A day in a man's life in 1920), in which the author attempts to imagine, "given this succession of inventions," what the life of a common man would be like within a decade. He envisages word systems based on abbreviations, underground trains, electric alarm clocks, airplanes, speed records, elevators, a "perpetual motion company," and a talking newspaper, which he goes on to describe: "The daily *Electro Fast*, with a daily circulation of 6 million home telephonographs, not counting the forty thousand information telephonographs on public squares, and the mammoth network joining major world capitals in colossal agencies" (Rio 1971: 71).

Thus we find in João do Rio's literary technique marks of the seductiveness of technology and of a foreseeable all-powerful future. One of these is the author's adoption of the genres that were privileged by the major newspapers of the turn of the century: reportage, interviews, and the *crônica*. Also, in his novels, stories, and plays, there is a marked mimetic relationship with journalistic language. An example of this is *A correspondência de uma estação de cura* (1918), which combines gossip and reportage in epistolary form on gambling, illicit deals, and nightspots in Poços de Caldas, a mountain resort town, while almost entirely suppressing the presence of the narrator as the organizing element of the events in the novel, fragmented in a series of short, autonomous epistolary narratives.

The case of Olavo Bilac is somewhat more contradictory. For about thirty years Bilac contributed to a large number of newspapers and magazines, such as *Gazeta Acadêmica, Cidade do Rio, Novidades, Correio do Povo, Gazeta de Notícias, Correio Mercantil, Correio Paulistano, O Estado de S. Paulo, República, A Notícia, Rio Nu, Mercúrio, A Cigarra, A Bruxa*, and *Kosmos*. Nevertheless, he seemed to hold in contempt not only his work as *cronista* (that is, a writer of *crônicas*) but also the newspaper public itself. Writes Bilac in *A Notícia*, in 1893: "After all, what are we all, journalists and *cronistas*, if not desecrators of art and journeymen of literature? Pure art is the refuge of an elite, a taste that few palates can savor. But mankind is no hothouse of superior souls" (Pontes 1944, 2: 551). This contempt sometimes extends to media other than the newspaper. Thus, in a 1907 *crônica* on the phonograph records sold at Casa Édison and the proliferation of phonographs on rua do Ouvidor (a street in downtown Rio known for its fashionable shops), Bilac wrote:

From every door comes the squeaky voice of a talking or singing machine; there are howls, moans, frantic quavers, oaths, yelps, cackling, meowing, barking, mooing, cooing, screams, shouts, grunts! And poor old rua do Ouvidor sounds like a gallery in hell, crowded with the souls of the damned, prisoners in cauldrons of boiling tar, mouthing curses and begging for mercy. (Meneses 1966: 355)

Elsewhere Bilac states that the cinematograph, the phonograph, and the changes then being experienced by the press were likely to cause men of letters to turn away from the press in the future. "Surely your days are numbered, O writers of *crônicas*, editorials, and news copy, and all other workers in written newspapers!" he exclaimed in *A Notícia*, predicting—but without João do Rio's fascination—the emergence of a "talking newspaper":

Soon we shall have the newspaper of the future, the talking and moving newspaper that will penetrate our eyes and ears more quickly, thanks to the combined action of phonographs and the Pathé films. Longer articles are already too trying for the attention span of the flighty public. Nearly all readers of dailies satisfy their curiosity by glancing through the dispatches, the shorter news items that sum up, in a few words, the latest goings-on in Congress, state secretariats, and the streets. (Pontes 1944, 2: 427)

Curiously, though, for all his rantings at the press, Bilac published most of his work in newspapers and magazines—serial novels such as *O esqueleto*, *Paula Matos*, and *Sanatorium*, hundreds of *crônicas* in prose or verse (such as his "Gazeta rimada" [Rhymed gazette]), and the sonnets of *Tarde* (1918), which first came out in the magazine *Careta*.

A comparison of two of the poems included in this posthumously published book—"A um poeta" and "O tear"—brings out the tension caused by the need to work for periodicals, with its own specific genres and forms of illustration (as in the magazines *A Cigarra* and *A Bruxa*, wholly written by Bilac and illustrated by Julião Machado), and the rejection of this kind of work, directly related to the new printing techniques and to a medium that favored superficiality, brevity, topicality, and inevitable redundancy. Bilac resorted to topicality in his serials and relied on a down-to-earth, satirical approach in his lighter *crônicas*, but in his texts with "artistic" pretensions the tone was quite different. In them there was a superabundance of apostrophes, showy language, recherché synonyms, and analogies with classical mythology; there was a clear effort to heighten the *difference* between these texts and his journalistic work, to contrast art with the technically produced images of photography and the movies, to leave aside the everyday topics that inspired his daily *crônicas*. This attempt at differentiation is most marked in Bilac's poetry.

There is an obvious contrast, for instance, between his Parnassian poetry and his advertisements in verse for Cruzeiro matches and Brasileira candles, or his "Canções do dia" (Songs of the day), inspired by everyday events, sung in the evening at the "Eden Concerto" by "the fat Yvonne." And this opposition can also be detected in his "artistic" verse, as for example in the two poems included in *Tarde* mentioned above: the weaver in "O tear" and the poet in "A um poeta" could not have been treated more differently. The "indifferent" weaver works "soullessly," "without haste, or pain, or joy," since the machine stands between him and the product of his work; the poet, however, who uses no machinery, creates "Beauty" with his bare hands, like a craftsman who "toils, and tries, and smoothes, and sweats, and suffers!" (Bilac 1919: 168–69). At a time marked by accelerated change and the desire for modernization—Bilac was in a privileged position to witness the introduction of new equipment in newspapers, and in 1917 he actually directed a scene in the movie *A pátria brasileira*—Bilac represents the ideal poet in the figure of the craftsman, one who works without relying on machinery.

The example of Lima Barreto, however, shows that Bilac's response is not the only possible one. In his work Lima Barreto also deals with the press and modern machinery, but though he always views them quite critically, this does not mean he can see good literature only as an antipode of journalism, as classical form, showy phraseology, rich and sonorous vocabulary—the distinguishing traits of Bilac's Parnassian verse.

Lima Barreto sometimes criticizes the proliferation of machines for the reproduction of sounds and images. In *Os bruzundangas* (1922), for instance, he satirizes the "bigwigs" of the Republic, observing that their "artistic culture" consists in "winding up the family gramophone" (Barreto 1985: 61). His references to newspapers are numerous and sometimes scathing, particularly when he mentions the leading papers of the day. Thus in *Recordações do escrivão Isaías Caminha* (1909) he mercilessly lampoons the workings of *O Globo* at the time. Again, in *Vida e morte de M. J. Gonzaga de Sá* (1919) there is devastating criticism of the major newspapers, magazines, and publishers of his day. "A newspaper, a large newspaper, you know very well what it is: a company of powerful people, who want to be flattered and who trust only those minds who are already duly recognized, notarized, rubber-stamped, and so forth," says Gonzaga de Sá to his friend Augusto Machado; "also, it takes many a deep bow to get to these large newspapers; and once you do, you have to throw away what is best in your brain, or you might shock the middle class and the bourgeoisie that make up their public" (Barreto n.d.: 47).[1] On the other hand, he is unconditionally sympathetic to "obscure magazines" and "fledgling newspapers."

Like his own character, Lima Barreto not only sympathized with small periodicals but also contributed to them—publications such as *Hoje*, *ABC*, and *A Lanterna*. This sympathy is again manifested in a *crônica* he published on February 14, 1920, on the seizure of an issue of the newspaper *A Folha*, owned by José Joaquim Medeiros e Albuquerque, on Rio's Avenida Central, a fact he associates with the persecution of the workers' publications *Spartacus* and *Plebe*. However, there was a difference: when Medeiros e Albuquerque's paper was confiscated, other newspapers protested; when the proletarian publications were persecuted, the press said nothing. Lima Barreto then asks: "Does this mean that only gentlemen, or would-be gentlemen, or near-gentlemen have the right to think and publish their thoughts? Does this mean that only the big papers are considered part of the Press?" (Barreto 1956: 253–54).

Thus Lima Barreto underscores the contrast between large and small newspapers; and his criticism of the press is consistent with his avoidance of the stylistic features that are characteristic of conventional journalese: topicality and showiness, for instance. In this he is the very opposite of Bilac, who relied on such effects with no qualms. Lima Barreto not only eschewed traditional journalistic devices but also reshaped them, for, as Isaías explains in *Recordações*, "In newspapers, writing is conceived of differently than in literature" (Barreto 1978: 186). "In newspapers, length is all, and the importance of a piece of writing is directly proportional to its size," the narrator of the novel observes; "the point is not to convey thoughts but to persuade readers by means of useless repetitions, and to impress them with the length of the article" (p. 186). For this reason, Lima Barreto finds it necessary to reshape journalistic resources before using them in literature. As Silviano Santiago observes, "Lima Barreto freed certain stylistic processes from the limits of the serial narrative, transforming them into resources for a popular aesthetics of the novel" (Santiago 1983: 94). Without relinquishing "redundancy" as a basic stylistic process,

Lima Barreto did without topicality and plot twists, then seen as inevitable devices in any text aiming at a wider public.

Reshaping in Lima Barreto; *mimesis* without qualms in João do Rio; *refusal* or embarrassed (but lucrative) assimilation in Bilac; and a perverse *displacement* of any marks of modernization in Rangel—these are no more than a few of the forms assumed by the dialogue between literary technique and the dissemination of new techniques in printing, reproduction, and broadcasting in turn-of-the-century Brazil.

What is clear, however, is that all literary producers in the Brazil of the period were forced to reckon with the new techniques of dissemination, though as yet hesitantly. At the time, according to Brito (1983), "the pressure of technical rationality in Brazil was still at an early stage. Science did not coordinate our reality, but it was a looming presence on the horizon. The encounter, the confrontation, was muted and latent, a silent process" (p. 15). It is this confrontation—sometimes covert, as in regionalist narratives, in "symbolist prose," and in most of the poetry of the period (whether Parnassian, symbolist, or penumbrista); sometimes explicit, as in João do Rio, Bilac, and Lima Barreto; sometimes almost silent, as in Godofredo Rangel or Léo Vaz—that I take as the starting point for a discussion of these three decades of literary production in Brazil.

Typical of these shifting views of the emblems of the modernization then being imposed on the country was the way some men of letters reacted to the exposition in celebration of the centennial of the opening of Brazilian harbors to all friendly nations, in Rio de Janeiro. Notes Hardman:

In 1908, on the occasion of the dazzling National Exposition in which the brand new republic outdid the comparable events of the old Empire in terms of pomp, neoclassicist splendor, and brilliant lighting, one could detect distinct representations by different writers of the time. (Hardman 1988: 95)

And he mentions as examples Bilac, a sort of official spokesman for the event, ideologically committed to it; João do Rio, the fascinated spectator of the modern *exhibitio*; and the anarchist Avelino Fóscolo, who criticized the expenses with the exhibition, which he found excessive. But whereas in this case Fóscolo was critical of a celebration of modernity, on other occasions leaders of the workers' movement gave their optimistic approval to whatever was seen as "progress." Here is one such example mentioned by Hardman: in 1901, members of the workers' organization Club Democrático Internacional Filhos do Trabalho, in São José do Rio Pardo, decided to send "enthusiastic congratulations to their fellow countryman Santos-Dumont," the Brazilian aviation pioneer, "for your discovery of the dirigibility of balloons, which is of incalculable consequences for the advent of socialism" (p. 95). This diversity of reactions—Bilac's approval, Fóscolo's restrictions, the optimism of workers, and the undisguised fascination of João do Rio—leads Hardman to see oscillation itself as a characteristic trait of the first attempts to understand this period of "transition to modernity." He writes: "This hesitation before the artifacts of modernity ultimately turns out to be the distinguishing mark of the new times, for all the differences between actual literary productions" (p. 95).

However, my intention is not merely to examine the Brazilian literature of the age of modernization from the angle of its conflicting feelings regarding the new technical horizons, but also to propose a history of Brazilian literature that considers its relationship with a history of the forms and means of communication, the innovations and transformations of which affect both the consciousness of authors and readers and the literary forms and representations themselves.

If, according to Gumbrecht, "each new medium in itself transforms the collective mentality, imprinting itself on the relationship people have to their bodies, consciousness, and actions" (1985: 212–13),[2] in the case of pre-modernist Brazil the almost simultaneous appearance of various new mechanisms (cinematograph, phonograph) and technical changes (from lithography to photography in newspaper printing, for instance) points to a significant transformation in the behaviors and perceptions of the people for whom these devices became objects of everyday use. For these decades—from the turn of the century to the 1920's—are indeed a privileged period for the study of the development of closer links between literature and the media. The first picture shows in Brazil took place in 1896; the first publication to regularly include illustrated ads, O Mercúrio, was started in 1898; the Edison phonograph was introduced in 1889; the use of photochemical methods of reproduction was pioneered by the Revista da Semana in 1900; color stereotyping was first used by the Gazeta de Notícias in 1907. All of these technical innovations were accompanied by changes in worldview and in perception, particularly among the populations of Rio de Janeiro, then the nation's capital, and other major Brazilian cities. And they left their traces on the cultural production, as I will attempt to demonstrate.

Admittedly, these traces are discontinuous, and perhaps their most typical form is the mixture of discomfort and fear with which most Brazilian writers of the time faced the typewriter.

There is a well-known *crônica* by Lima Barreto titled "Esta minha letra ... ," published in the *Gazeta da Tarde* on June 18, 1911, in which the author discussed the innumerable typographical and proofreading errors to be found in his serials, which he attributed to his illegible handwriting. Lima Barreto was given all sorts of advice: some asked him to change his handwriting, while others suggested that he use a typewriter. But this suggestion the author found unthinkable: "Leaving aside the matter of the cost of these graceless machines, let me simply remind the readers that typing is a wearisome affair and forces me to undertake the disgusting task of doing an article twice: writing it longhand and then making a type-written fair copy of it" (Barreto 1956: 295).

The possibility of typing without a previous handwritten draft was simply unimaginable. It is as though writing could not be conceived of except as a manual activity, a sort of craftsmanship; typing was possible only after composition was finished, to make a fair copy. And this task Lima Barreto found "disgusting."

Godofredo Rangel was just as unwilling to use the typewriter, as is indicated in the letters Monteiro Lobato addressed to him. From September 22, 1909, Lobato kept asking his friend to type his letters: "How awful your handwriting is—worse than mine even! Really, we ought to get typewriters" (Lobato 1968, 1: 275). In later letters, however, Lobato him-self sometimes expressed feelings similar to Lima Barreto's: to him, the typewriter served only to make fair copies of handwritten texts. But unlike Lima Barreto, he seemed to enjoy typing. "I've finished typing all the letters," he wrote on October 27, 1943, "and now I'm reading the whole batch" (Lobato 1968, 2: 360). Two years later, thinking about publishing his correspondence, he asked Rangel: "People are always ask-ing about your letters. Well, are you sure you're not up to it? Haven't you typed and polished them yet?" (p. 367). Rangel still seemed uninterested. And to encourage his friend to publish *Vida ociosa*, Lobato felt it necessary to proclaim the advantages of the printed word, in a letter dated August 30, 1916: "The good thing about publishing *Vida* in a magazine is finally being able to see it in print, so you can give it the final touches. When a book is in manuscript you don't have a real view of it" (p. 102).

While Rangel silently ignored his friend's insistence that he use a typewriter, Lobato's letters stressed the inevitability of the replacement of "calligraphic writing"[3] with a less immediate relation between literary producers and their texts; and the mediator was the typewriter, the type-written text. Given this situation, and the entire technical context that had been taking shape in Brazil since the late nineteenth century, writers seemed to become gradually aware that the substitution of the mechanical gesture of typing for the act of writing by hand would be followed by an inevitable confrontation with the various modern artifacts and also by the death of a view of literature as a kind of highly personalized handicraft. This, in part, was why writers hesitated before adopting the regular use of the typewriter—and also why their attitude was so changeable about the various implications for literature of the dialogue between writing and technology—muted at first, but growing more and more important since the turn of the century.

CHAPTER 3

The Traces of Technology

The technological context that was often to interact with literary production in Brazil began around the late 1880's. It included the expansion of the railroad network (in 1885, there were 7,602 kilometers in use, 2,268 kilometers were under construction, and 5,060 more were planned); the use of electrical lighting in theaters (this began in Rio de Janeiro's Teatro Lucinda, where a steam generator was installed in 1887); the systematic adoption of electric streetcars (undertaken by the Botanical Garden Company in Rio in 1894); the appearance of the first balloons and airplanes; the growing numbers of automobiles in the largest cities (in Rio, six cars were in circulation in 1903, thirty-five in 1906). The decisive factors in this process were the diffusion of photography, the telephone, motion pictures, and the phonograph, as well as the introduction of new techniques of sound recording, printing and reproduction of texts, drawings, and photographs, and the expansion of advertising.

Before analyzing the impact of the new technologies on literary form in the 1890's and early twentieth century, however, it is important to date the appearance and diffusion of the apparatuses directly or indirectly involved in this interchange. First I discuss the literary and nonliterary records of the dissemination of these techniques and examine how these industrial artifacts were represented in literary works. Then I attempt to analyze some of the ways in which the intensification of the contact with these changes and modern devices was not only the object of description and discussion but also began to shape the technique of certain authors.

Kodaks and Ornaments

A good point of departure is photography. Its emergence in Brazil had taken place much earlier: in 1833, if one thinks of the pioneer Hercule Florence, or 1839, if one considers the first daguerreotypes to circulate in the empire. But before tracing the history of photography in Brazil, I must recount a story told by Kossoy (1980: 25), who found it in Scharf 1986, who in turn had it from the second volume of Grandville 1842.

In Louis Viardot's parable (illustrated by Grandville), which will sound quite cruel to Brazilian readers, Topaze, a local monkey artist, goes to Paris to perfect his art. But he gives up his career as portrait painter when he finds that what is required of him is imagination rather than imitation. He decides to buy a device for making daguerreotypes and returns to Brazil, where he opens the first photography studio in the country. Photo portraits are suddenly all the rage, and "everyone in jungle society" wants one. The monkey daguerreotype artist becomes increasingly successful. But a jealous king destroys his studio, and Topaze finally throws himself in the Amazon.

The real target of this little story is not Brazil but the many painters who were becoming photographers with the growth of daguerreotypy in Europe. And the distinction between "creating" and "imitating" had more to do with this change than with Brazilians' supposed lack of capacity for anything more than imitation. In the story, Brazil is no more than an exotic, wild backdrop for an account of the dissemination of the processes for the mechanical recording of images in European society—with, of course, a passing snipe at Brazilian artists studying in Europe and their dependence on European masters.

If Brazilians were indeed doomed to ape Europeans, one should expect technical processes of reproduction to be wholeheartedly welcomed in late-nineteenth-century Brazil. But one need only think of Bilac's disapproval of phonographs and of his own hack work for the press—counterbalanced by unrestricted praise for such shows of Brazilian "progress" as the 1908 exposition—to realize that in Brazilian society the establishment of a technical perspective was neither as fast nor as consensual as it was in Topaze's "jungle society."

In particular, the actual history of daguerreotypy in Brazil was quite different from what Grandville's parable might suggest. It was never very popular in the country, nor was there any jealousy on the part of the emperor. Quite the contrary, there were very few daguerreotypists active in Brazil in the 1840's and 1850's, and Pedro II was an enthusiastic defender of photography—in fact, he himself experimented with daguerreotypy.[1]

"The 1847 almanac published by the Laemmert brothers," writes Kossoy, "mentions the existence of no more than three active daguerreotypists in Rio de Janeiro, though there were probably other pioneers at work, if only on a temporary basis" (1980: 30). And already in the 1850's daguerreotypy—which could produce a single, nonreproducible image—was being abandoned in favor of new photographic processes that made it possible to print a number of copies on paper from a single negative. Thus it was only in the 1860's that photography began to achieve true popularity in Brazil.

But on March 13, 1864, Henrique Fleiuss published a cartoon in *Semana Ilustrada* titled "Fotografia malograda" (A frustrated photograph), which suggests that much of the population remained unfamiliar with the new technique. The first panel shows a photographer telling a group of people about to be photographed: "Don't be afraid, my dear fellows, this won't hurt; just let me count one … two … three, and your portrait will be ready." He counts: "One … two … ," and the second panel shows that the frightened group has already dispersed before he can count three (Kossoy 1980: 41).

It was in this period that photography studios began to proliferate, particularly in Rio. Writes Kossoy:

In 1863, thirty studios were advertising their services in the city, many of them still owned by foreigners.

By this time they were more securely established, clearly because the market had grown. And this growing market was formed by the rise of a new clientele, which took its place alongside the official nobility, the rural gentry, and the wealthier businessmen, a class made up of a significant number of middle-class persons: military officers, priests, public servants, artists, teachers, professionals, and others. (Kossoy 1980: 41)

More photographers' studios were opened, and new genres of photography arose that popularized the new medium: the calling card, the photopainting, and—in the late 1870's—the "life-size portraits" made with a "solar camera."

And if in the 1850's a decisive innovation had occurred—the single image produced by daguerreotypy had been replaced by the countless copies made possible with the advent of the negative-positive process—

other significant changes came in the 1880's. "The use of albumenized paper for copies went into slow decline with the introduction of the new silver chloride or bromide gelatin papers, which were much more sensitive," Kossoy explains. And he adds that "in 1882 Alberto Henschel was already using gelatin-coated dry plates," for in this year Henschel announced: "We can make instant portraits of very young children" (Kossoy 1980: 81).

Two decades later, in 1901, the postcard was introduced in Brazil; it was to be an important medium for the dissemination of photography. Another major vehicle was the photo album, with views of various cities and states, a good example of which is Augusto Malta's Rio de Janeiro album, published in 1911. By this time phototypy had been introduced in the press, a number of illustrated magazines had appeared, and photos were common in drug advertising, so that Brazilians were taking photography for granted. A significant sign of this popularization is the growing number of amateur photographers. Gonzaga Duque alludes to this phenomenon in passing in "A estética das praias" (1910) when he suggests that policemen in charge of beaches should look out for "insolent persons" who "raise their voices" or even "make violent gestures" when some lady is strolling, rather than concentrate on the photographers that are sometimes seen there:

And the policeman who hastens to stop the amateur photographer from taking a "snapshot" of a girl emerging from the waves, in response to the alarm of the foolish relative escorting her, would do better to shoo away those violent beasts who dress according to the latest fashions. (Estrada 1910: 156)

With the increase in the number of amateur photographers there appeared, in 1910, their first association, the Photo Clube of Rio de Janeiro, and, in 1909, the first magazine specializing in photography, the *Revista Photographica*, in São Paulo.

According to Herkenhoff, despite the relationship of photography with the "fine arts," the popularization of photography in Brazil did not affect the painting technique of the Imperial Academy, but it may explain a certain limitation in the themes used in academic painting:

In nineteenth-century Brazil a compromise occurred. Painting was the province of idealized imagery, impossible to capture by mechanical means: patriotic allegory, historical and religious themes ("The Last of the Tamoyo," "First Mass in Brazil," "Samson and Delilah"), following a differentiated treatment, but always within the bounds of the academic repertoire. Photography was, for the most part, concerned with documenting reality. (Herkenhoff 1983: 40)

Thus the typical subjects of paintings were historical and mythological scenes—the three examples mentioned by Herkenhoff are respectively by Rodolfo Amoedo, Vítor Meireles de Lima, and Oscar Pereira da Silva. But concentration on such themes was not the only way Brazilian painting responded to the challenge posed first by photography and then—beginning in 1896—by motion pictures, not to mention the inevitable changes in perception brought about by stereoscopes, photographic albums of views, postcards, portraits, biographs, kinetoscopes, and later the omniograph and the cinematograph.

But in Vítor Meireles's panoramas, in the sun-drenched landscapes of Roberto Mendes, in Almeida Júnior's scenes of rural life, in the concern with light evident in canvases by Georgina de Albuquerque such as "Dia de sol," "Canto do rio," or "Vaso de cristal," in the blurred contours of Belmiro de Almeida's "Efeitos de sol" and "Bom tempo," in the dispersed luminosity of Eliseu Visconti's plein-air paintings, one finds a different kind of dialogue with the photographic image. What these works suggest is an attempt to take into account, in the technique of painting, the redefinition of perception and vision brought about by the new technical developments of the late nineteenth century, by means of such devices as lighting effects, short brushstrokes, and the deemphasizing of boundaries.

An intelligent solution was found in the sphere of photography itself by Valério Vieira in his photomontage "Os trinta Valérios," produced between 1890 and 1900, which earned him a silver medal in the 1904 Louisiana Purchase Exposition. At first, one sees what seems to be an ordinary scene. A group of musicians perform before a small audience, while a few other spectators appear in the background, being served drinks by a servant. After a while, however, one realizes that everyone—the musicians, the spectators (even a latecomer still on the stairs), the portraits on the wall, a bust on a piece of furniture, the white-capped servant—has the same face, the face of Valério Vieira; they are the "thirty Valérios" referred to in the title.

Just as painting attempted to find alternatives to allegory and historical themes, photography tried—at least this once—to question the aura of "objectivity" and the mission of "documentation" that had been attributed to it. "The 'magic' of the thirty Valérios also questions the sight of each human being," writes Herkenhoff. "The mechanical eye is able to capture immediately an image that is refused by intelligence" (Herkenhoff 1983: 41). In this way, the blind faith in technically produced images was challenged.

"The seemingly nonsymbolic, objective character of technically produced images leads the observer to see them as windows rather than as images," notes Flusser (1985: 20). "One trusts technically produced images as much as one trusts one's own eyes." However, "technically produced images are not windows but *images*, surfaces that transcode processes into scenes" (p. 21). Herein lies the importance of Valério Vieira's play with information, with the gesture of photographing and the possibility of making anything "real," at the very moment when photography was beginning to gain a foothold in Brazil: he provided a more critical view of the photographic process by means of the process itself.

But "Os trinta Valérios" was an exception. The visual delight in photography, the belief in the apparent "evidence" furnished by any photographed scene, was the rule. Thus it was that in turn-of-the-century Brazil, newspapers, illustrated magazines, and the nascent advertising "industry" were all fascinated by technically produced images.

The growing influence of photography is evident, for instance, in Gonzaga Duque's review of an exhibition of works by José Malhoa, reprinted in *Graves & frívolos* (1910):

Relying on the fundamental secrets of the palette and considerable practice in the difficult art of drawing, in almost every case he captures the observed subjects in all their undisturbed naturalness. It is as if he Kodaked them. And thanks to this power of retention, his images, whatever they may be, are alive in the paintings. (Estrada 1910: 40)

This inescapable dialogue between technically produced images and painted images would later be extended to the language of journalism and literary production. Comments Flusser: "Throughout history, texts had explained images, *demythifying* them. From then on, images would illustrate texts, *remythifying* them" (Flusser 1985: 62). This he exemplifies with the case of the reader of a newspaper. "One may resort to the text accompanying the photograph in order to name the image one sees, but while reading the article one is under the magical spell of photography and does not want an explanation, but rather a mere confirmation, of what one has seen" (p. 63).

This subordination of the text to the image was to be characteristic of turn-of-the-century Brazilian illustrated magazines. Writing about *Kosmos* magazine (1904–1909) in *Tempos eufóricos*, Dimas observes that the editors were so "fascinated by the expressive possibilities of photography and color printing" that they "attempted to illustrate everything, so that the written text was often relegated to a quite secondary plane" (Dimas 1983: 5). This clearly left a mark on the articles, *crônicas*, and short stories published in the magazine.

The writers who contributed to *Kosmos* were themselves aware of this fact. Silva Marques wrote, in an article published in March 1909 titled "O domínio da gravura" (The domination of illustration), that "a day will come when even a doctrinal article will rely on illustrations, portraying the idea it attacks as a monstrous figure and the idea it propounds as a contrasting form" (Dimas 1983: 8). Hence the obsessive use of a rich vocabulary, of emphatic wording, of dramatic and ornamental rhetoric. It is as though language, facing the increasing eminence of images, resorted to hyperbole, excessive ornamentation, and preciosity.

This taste for ornamentation was opposed, however, by writers like Pedro Kilkerry, particularly in his *crônicas* "Quotidianas" and "Kodaks" (an apt name, underscoring the analogy between the journalist text and the snapshot), published in Bahia's *Jornal Moderno* in 1913. Kilkerry's "notes on local life" are indeed suggestive of a snapshot in their quick, direct manner. A good example of his style is given by a *crônica* in which he describes an evening at the Ideal movie theater, published on March 8, 1913:

No more, no less ...

A nervously dark gentleman, *ojos criollos*, decided, it seems, to *savor* the morbid, though subtle, delight of pinching someone near him (the motive, others say, was more frivolous).

Soon the whole room shook, heard a democratic "No!" and finally settled on a stronger emotion, at the distinct sound of a redress.

A hand, white but used to automatic brakes, elicited a resonance from the very tropical dark gentleman's face, who was suddenly eclipsed by one of the exits of the Ideal ... (Campos 1985: 172)

The situation is described in three bright flashes. First, the gentleman with *ojos criollos* (criollo eyes) pinches someone; second, everyone in the theater is surprised; third, the dark gentleman is slapped and escapes: three snapshots in three short paragraphs. And these paragraphs are surprising not only because of the wording, or of the choice of subjects of each action—the "nervously dark gentleman," "the whole room," and "a white hand"—but also because of the quick succession of images.

Kilkerry converses with technique and, in a critical mimesis, transforms narrative technique. His *crônica* is not a quasi-diary full of confessions and personal impressions, or a display of precious language and flights of rhetoric; it does not attempt to compete with the illustration and has no use for ornament. Kilkerry takes from technology what will work for him. He opts for a drier, more concise language, one that reflects the awareness of the urgency and the spatial constraints of the newspaper.

In one of his "Quotidianas," Kilkerry writes of the noise of the presses and about what it is to write under constant pressure:

As I write these words, the typographer casts his sweaty, urgent eye on them, and I can hear the eager trepidation of the press, with which I associate the eagerness of our readers, of their social moment, their time. (Campos 1985: 167)

Thus Kilkerry writes in the presence of this eager trepidation and of all this new machinery. His words are reminiscent of other snapshot-like texts, such as Alcântara Machado's *Pathé Baby* (1926) and certain passages in Oswald de Andrade's *Serafim Ponte Grande* (1933)—both, however, were published after the 1922 Week of Modern Art, and displayed, two decades after Kilkerry's "Kodaks," a sophisticated interchange with the new technologies. Here is one example from *Pathé Baby*, a description by means of snapshots:

Noise. Dust. And people. Lots of people. The cop blows his whistle, raises his staff, the traffic stops so that the nurse and her baby carriage may cross the street unhurriedly. And two little seamstresses talking nonstop. A family on its way to the sleepy benches of the Bois. A one-armed man selling pins. The laughter of a blonde with green rings around her eyes. An Englishman's Kodak. Two lovers. Israelites showing off their Legion d'Honneur rosettes. Monocles. Paris passes. (Machado 1983, 2: 65)

The text seems even sparer, without the sequence of surprises in Kilkerry's "Kodaks," but with some brilliant syntheses, such as "Paris passes" at the end. This was possible in part because a few Brazilian writers in the 1920's resumed the confrontation between literature and technology that had begun, somewhat hesitantly, in the late nineteenth century. But photography was only one of the new techniques.

"Perfect Illusion"

This dialogue was intensified in the 1890's with the advent of the cinematograph and the mechanical reproduction of movement. Here is a detailed description of a kinetoscope show, published in the Rio daily *Jornal do Brasil* on December 9, 1894:

The day before yesterday, at rua do Ouvidor, 131, the kinetoscope was unveiled. This is Edison's latest invention, and like all of the creations of this learned and prolific inventor, it is a wonder.

We saw a cockfight with all its thrills, the spectators' cheers and enthusiastic gestures. Then we saw a serpentine dance, correctly done, and finally a curious fight in a tavern. (Ferreira 1986: 17)

This was followed by an equally detailed description of the functioning of the kinetoscope, as if at that time modern machinery were itself a spectacle as interesting as a movie:

The kinetoscope consists of a film with 150 images rotating one thousand times a second. This film, a plate exposed at an extraordinary speed so as to capture all the movements to be represented, is set in motion by a 20-volt engine.

This kinetoscope is worth a visit, for it is not only quite interesting in itself but also a novelty to us. (Ferreira 1986: 17)

It was not the cockfights or the dance that should be seen but the mechanism itself. The real attraction was the technique. That is why the first advertisements of the cinematograph gave little emphasis to the actual sights reproduced. What was important was that the new apparatus was technically superior to the kinetoscope. Urbano Duarte wrote in the *Jornal do Commercio* on June 21, 1896:

I am told that soon we are to have an opportunity to wonder at the cinematograph, one of the marvels of this turn of the century. We have all seen Edison's kinetoscope, which reproduces movement by displaying to the eye a quick succession of instant photographs. But in the kinetoscope the images were tiny, and only one person at a time could see them. The cinematograph, invented by the Lumière brothers, shows us life-size figures that can be seen by any number of spectators. (Ferreira 1986: 17)

From the tiny images seen by a single eye to life-size images shown before audiences of up to 200 people, the change involved an increase in the size not only of the pictures but also of the potential public. This implied a major change in forms of perception, at least in the principal Brazilian cities.

On July 8, 1896, in Rio, the cinematograph was shown for the first time in Brazil, to an audience of special guests and newspapermen in a room on rua do Ouvidor. This momentous occasion was reported by the *Jornal do Commercio* on the following day:

In an ample rectangular room, lighted by electric Edison lightbulbs, with walls painted dark red, there are about two hundred chairs, regularly arranged in lines, all facing the back wall, where a reflecting screen, about 2 meters wide, has been placed at the appropriate height. The apparatus is behind the spectators, in a small closed cabinet between the two entrance doors. The electric lights are extinguished, the room plunges into darkness, and on the screen the lighted projection is seen, at first only a vague fixed image, which little by little becomes sharper. When the apparatus begins to function, the figures are seen to move. (Ferreira 1986: 18)

All of this was to become routine in a few years, but in 1896 everything, from the position of the projector or the screen to the darkness in the room, seemed new and unknown. That is why the article ends with a warning "against pickpockets," for "the darkness that prevails during the session," says the *Jornal do Commercio*, "does much in the way of helping them ply their trade of harvesting fruit that belongs to others" (p. 18).

Thus it was with a combination of caution and wonderment at the "magnificent impression of real life" that the cinematograph was received at first in Brazil—more wonderment than caution, in fact. On August 7 and 8, 1896, the first picture shows took place in São Paulo; on July 31, 1897, the Salão Novidades Paris was opened in Rio; and in 1898 Brazilian filmmaking began, when the first picture shows were filmed in Brazil (Araújo 1976).[2]

After the official opening of avenida Central, the major thoroughfare in downtown Rio, on November 15, 1905, other movie theaters appeared. "The time had come for stabilization of movie theaters, now bigger, more comfortable, and prepared to receive a more numerous audience," observes Araújo (1976: 18). Beginning in 1907, new cinemas mushroomed: the Parisiense, the Pathé, the Paraíso do Rio, the Pavilhão Internacional, the Moderno, the Odeon, the Avenida, the Universal Animatographo, the Éclair-Palace, the Ideal, the Soberano, the Chantecler (Vieira and Pereira 1986: 25). This proliferation of theaters—encouraged from 1910 on by the industrialization of electric power in Rio and São Paulo—explains the appearance of ads such as the following, published in the *Gazeta de Notícias* on April 2, 1905: "Electricity / General applications / R. Joyeux / Electrical engineer, graduated from Escola de Torpedos and a former officer in the French Navy. / Installation of cinematographic equipment. / Office and store: rua Senador Dantas, 44 / Workshop: rua Evaristo da Veiga, 38" (Xavier 1978: 120). And the public must have been large, since theater owners sold space in the curtains of projection rooms to various advertisers. The Maison Moderne placed the following ad in the *Gazeta de Notícias* on January 22, 1907: "Today, the new curtain is to be installed. We request the presence of all our distinguished advertisers."

In this way, the itinerant picture shows of the 1890's were gradually replaced by more stable circumstances for the exhibition and production of movies. From 1908 to 1911 Brazilian filmmaking was especially prolific. During this period, "since the international market had not yet become as organized and monopolistic as it did after the Great War," writes Xavier (1978: 121), "it was possible for locally produced movies to get shown; in fact, they accounted for a generous share of the market."

Of these Brazilian-made movies, which found an interested public, some were documentaries—*A festa campestre de famílias cariocas* (The fête champêtre of Carioca families) and such Carnival films as *O corso de Botafogo* and *O carnaval de 1908 no Rio*—and others were close to crime reportage, such as Marc Ferrez's *A mala sinistra* (The sinister suitcase) and Antônio Leal's *Os estranguladores do Rio* (The Rio stranglers, 1908), one of the most successful movies of the period; there were fiction films, such as Eduardo Leite and Américo Colombo's *A viúva alegre* (The merry widow, 1909), and José do Patrocínio Filho's revue *Paz e amor* (Peace and love, 1910), according to Vicente de Paula Araújo "the most popular Brazilian movie of the first two decades of the century" (Araújo 1976: 356).

The advent of sound did much for the popularity of films. Rio's newspapers began enthusiastically anticipating the coming of talkies in 1904, and on November 22 the *Gazeta de Notícias* announced that a "talking cinematograph" was to be shown to the public. The new contraption was the property of Edouard Hervet, who described it as "an apparatus of perfect illusion," a veritable "marvel of its kind." But not until 1908 did the new development come into wider use. This was made possible by new machines that synchronized phonographs and cinematographs: the chronophone, the cinephono, the synchrophone, and the synchronoscope.

Often, according to Araújo, "actors or singers would hide behind the screen to speak and sing in synch with the pictures" (1976: 230). The approval of sound in movies was not unanimous. Though talkies were popular, they were condemned by some, like Sebastião Sampaio, a critic for *Gazeta de Notícias*, who wrote, on July 31, 1910: "I much prefer the cinematograph without the phonograph. Has the reader seen the revue *Paz e amor*? And did not the reader experience a certain unease? Does not the exact rendering of life, with all its voices and noises, detract from the enchantment, the sweet illusion of movies?" (p. 343).

The introduction of sound via the phonograph, however, had the effect of investing silent films with a new allure: they were full of "enchantment." This view was contrary to the common wisdom of the time, which held that movies were mere entertainment, not "art." In a cartoon published by J. Carlos in the magazine *Careta* on December 11, 1909, captioned "Advertisement for an art movie," a "swell" talks to a family about the "art movie" he has seen: "Well, you shouldn't miss it . . . It is an excellent film . . . The Prince falls in love with a peasant girl . . . In short, it is a drama that may be enjoyed by the most mediocre minds" (p. 285). In this way, J. Carlos mocks the very notion of such a thing as an "art movie."

This is why movies, in their first decade in Brazil, were usually mentioned simply as news or advertised. At the most, they were discussed from a moral perspective, or as to their influence (pernicious or not) on other areas of cultural production. It was only in the late 1910's that the first critical comments on films and specialized movie magazines appeared. In Rio de Janeiro, the magazines were *A Fita, Palcos e Telas, Para Todos . . .* , *Scena Muda,* and *A Tela*; in São Paulo's edition of *A Fita,* Antônio Campos published his reflections on cinema (Xavier 1978: 126–30).

It was also in the 1910's that it became more common for men of letters to take an active part in the promising new Brazilian movie industry. In 1917, Bilac directed a part of *A pátria brasileira* (The Brazilian fatherland). Coelho Neto wrote the script for the unfinished serial *Os mistérios do Rio de Janeiro* (The mysteries of Rio de Janeiro, 1915). And Bastos Tigre wrote rhyming subtitles for *O filme do diabo* (The devil's movie, 1915), a few of which have survived: "Again the fighting grows fiercer / An intense, unequal fight / And Susana then swoons / In the officer's arms," or "Among spurts of machine-gun fire / From the friendly trench emerges / A soldier who attempts / To save the maiden's life" (Machado Neto 1973: 223). Through simple, stressed sound patterns and short lines, Tigre attempts to follow the swift flow of images and describe the action in a relatively straightforward way.

But usually writers had a more indirect relation with movies. Mostly they tended to discuss films in their *crônicas* and fiction works rather than write for the movie industry. In any case, beginning in 1912 Brazilian filmmakers concentrated on documentaries, while fiction increasingly became the province of imported products.

So to Brazilian authors the movies were more a topic to write about than a market to write for. For instance, in Léo Vaz's *O professor Jeremias*

(1920) the cinematograph is mentioned solely as a pretext for introducing another argument between Dona Antoninha and Jeremias (the narrator):

We were about to go to the cinematograph; I observed that you, my son, being far too young, would only sleep there, as usual, and therefore it made more sense to leave you at home. Whereupon Dona Antoninha replied:
   "Leave him here?! And who is to look after him? That is all very well for people who have nurses." (Vaz 1920: 232)

If in Vaz's novel the movies are the spark that cause a quarrel, in a well-known *crônica* by Lima Barreto they are a topic for conversation for people in the "suburb train" early in the afternoon:

At this time, no longer does the train smell of politics, rises in wages, or bureaucratic problems; rather, there is a rich scent of motion pictures. It's Gaumont this and Nordisk that, and Fatty Arbuckle and Theda Bara and God knows what else! (Barreto 1956: 245)

Such passing references to the cinematographer suggest that by the 1910's and 1920's the new device had become an everyday form of entertainment. But some mentions were critical. In João do Rio's epistolary novel *A correspondência de uma estação de cura* (1918), Teodomiro writes his friend Godofredo de Alencar about going to the Politeama in Poços de Caldas to see *A filha do circo*. He notes: "While watching the movie, in respectful silence, I pondered over the impossibility of setting limits to human stupidity. *A filha do circo* is simply staggering" (Rio 1918: 149). But João do Rio was not always dismissive of movies. In another novel, *A profissão de Jacques Pedreira* (1911), he describes a biograph in the most enthusiastic terms.

   In fact, João do Rio tended to write glowingly of modern inventions and techniques, and in such a way as to make it plain that he was aware of the dramatic change they caused in the very "way of looking." The author began to think of his activity as a *cronista* in terms of an analogy with filmmaking. So it was that he titled his 1909 volume of *crônicas Cinematógrafo*. In this book, he praises the cinematograph's potential for the making of documentaries, while at the same time redefining the object of documentaries—life—as "a huge cinematograph," in which "every man has a cinematograph in his skull, operated by imagination": "one need only close one's eyes to see the movies unraveling in one's cortex at an unbelievable speed" (Rio 1909: viii).

   A cinematograph in one's skull: with this trope João do Rio seems to capture the triumph of an absentminded and fragmentary kind of attention of readers and spectators. "Reception through distraction, which is increasingly conspicuous in all domains of art and is a symptom of profound changes in perceptive structures, finds its privileged locus in film" writes Benjamin (1985, 1: 194). In his own way João do Rio was aware of these changes. "That was an interesting movie, you say. And two minutes later you have forgotten it," he wrote (Rio 1909: vi). It did not seem to matter if one saw only a fragment or paid little attention to the pictures shown. For "those who are there to watch the movie show do not feel they are under any obligation to believe what they see is important, or to give their definitive opinion" (p. vii); one might well "walk out during the show with no qualms and try to find amusement elsewhere" (p. v). The cinematograph itself suggested the possibility of quick disposal, of absentminded reception, of superficiality:

> The screen, the dark room, the projection, the operator turning the handle—and here are streets, beggars, politicians, actresses, follies, merrymaking, agony, divorce, hunger, feasts, triumphs, defeats, a huge crowd, the entire city, a human flood—and all they do is make a few gestures and then disappear without a trace, without letting themselves be penetrated. (P. vi)

It was this aspect of the cinematograph that interested João do Rio: its ability to pass without leaving a trace. His characters are purposely superficial, almost like figures in a fashion magazine: the dramatis personae of *Chá das 5*, the many visitors at Poços de Caldas in *A correspondência de uma estação de cura*, the various kinds of social climbers in *A profissão de Jacques Pedreira*. The same fascination for what passes "without letting [itself] be penetrated" is evident in his interest in the *crônica*—which João do Rio thought of as a form akin to the movies. In the opening text of his *Cinematógrafo*, he writes:

> The *crônica* evolves toward the cinematograph. It was once reflection and commentary, the reverse of this sinister, unclassifiable animal known as the editorial. It turned into illustration and caricature. Later it was a retouched photograph, albeit a living one. With the frenetic hurry of us all, it is now cinematographic—a cinematograph of words, the novel of the projectionist in the labyrinth of facts, of other people's lives, and fantasy—but a novel in which the projectionist is a secondary character dragged along by the rush of events. (Rio 1909: x)

The writer of *crônicas* as projectionist, the *crônicas* as movies, the book of *crônicas* as a cinematograph of words: these are the analogies on which *Cinematógrafo* is built; this is how João do Rio perceived his own activity as *cronista*. The comparison to movies may suggest a weakening of the figure of the narrator ("a secondary character dragged along by the rush of events"). This is made clear, for instance, by the fragmented structure of his epistolary novel *A correspondência*, in which there is no single narrator but instead a series of brief narratives, each told by a different character. It also suggests a preference for two-dimensional characters. But it does not imply a substantial transformation in João do Rio's texts. His relationship with the new technical developments is basically one of enchantment, as the *crônicas* indicate, of a mimesis that attempts to be literal but involves only some of the features of the new techniques. That is why he attempts to think of the *crônica* as movies or to create characters that are almost all surface.

This desire for mimesis and this connection established more through analogy than through literary language suggest that João do Rio was somewhat dazzled by the new technological devices and attempted to imagine ways of responding to them. And just as he dreams, in a 1910 *crônica*, of a "daily *Electro Fast*," he presents the image of a "cinematograph of words" to signal a literature that would function similarly to the modern apparatuses for the production and reproduction of technical images. Thus his somewhat startled initial response is to attempt to mimic the new devices. To João do Rio, it does not yet seem possible to reelaborate on the new inventions critically; the most he can do is flirt with them. But he was not the only writer of his time to react in this way. In fact, most authors from the 1890's to the early 1920's seemed hesitant about the new technical world and shrank from developing dangerous liaisons with the modern apparatuses, just as they failed to arrive at results that were aesthetically more satisfying.

It was only with the rise of modernist prose that montage and cuts became common in literary technique. Brazilian fiction "lost the syntax of the heart and its trousers," as Oswald de Andrade puts it in *Serafim Ponte Grande* (1933), only in such texts as his own *Serafim* and *Memórias sentimentais de João Miramar* (1924), Mário de Andrade's *Macunaíma* (1928) and Alcântara Machado's *Pathé Baby*. Here indeed is a cinematic literature, attuned to a different conception of cinema, and unconcerned with any attempt to be read like a film or to mention the biograph or the cinematograph; a literature that is no longer under the impact of surprise, that converses ironically with the new techniques and forms of perception, that feels no need to mention motion pictures obsessively but instead appropriates the elements of filmmaking that interest it and redefines them according to its own purposes.

Klaxons, Pianos, and Phonographs

But when João do Rio attempts to characterize the "cinematographic man" who is coming into being simultaneously with modern technology, he does not mention only the cinematograph. "All the discoveries of the past two decades have had the effect of speeding up the pace of existence," he observes in a 1908 *crônica*, "the automobile, this delightful invention; the phonograph, this torment that shortens distances and preserves voices so that no time will be lost—these are indeed the symbols of our times" (Rio 1909: 386). To him, the distinguishing feature of what he calls *"Homus cinematographicus"* is haste. "What is the basic aim of us all? To get it over with quickly! Cinematographic man has opted for the supreme folly: filling time, burdening time, cramming time quite full, paralyzing time in order to overtake it" (p. 388).

To João do Rio, this attempt to paralyze time includes not only the new techniques of production and reproduction of images and sounds but also the modern possibilities of locomotion in such vehicles as trains, electric streetcars, and automobiles. These devices made it possible to overcome distances, hitherto seemingly enormous, thanks to mechanical vehicles—and also to control time, since one could now lengthen it or shorten it depending on whether one used the new means of transportation.

It makes sense, then, that the automobile should function as a sort of mechanical protagonist in such works as João do Rio's *A profissão*. It is in a car that the romance between Jacques and Alice dos Santos, wife of the politician Arcanjo, begins; the automobile serves as a moving stage for the affair, and also hints at the short duration of the liaison. It is worth noting that Jacques's expert handling of the auto's mechanical contraptions parallels his self-confidence as a lover:

Any word would have been useless—with a quick gesture Jacques pulled down the blinds, picked up the speaking tube and said "Slow down!," embraced her with the violence of his triumphant adolescence. . . . And the automobile slowly klaxoned down the street, threatening the passersby. It was six-thirty in the afternoon. (Rio 1911: 78–79)

Terms related to the automobile—speaking tube and klaxon—are associated with the description of the love scene, just as mechanical movement is equated with the mechanics of seduction.

But an automobile race involving a bet made by Jorge de Araújo and Teotônio Filho, which culminates in the tragic death of Jorge's chauffeur, causes an important change in the hero's fate. After Jacques witnesses the bet, the race, and the death and is featured unsympathetically in the press coverage of the accident, the influence of his family and Alice dos Santos's requests directed at her husband, partly in order to get him out of sight, have the effect of securing a diplomatic post for Jacques abroad. He gets the job, after a half-hearted but ultimately successful effort that is mediated by the automobile, ever present in his affairs, whether professional or of the heart.

As Meneses observes, when the automobile arrived "it took over the city." In 1903 the city issued six private-car licenses. Meneses notes:

Whereas in 1904 seven private automobiles had been licensed, there were twelve in the following year and 35 in 1906. It was then that the first affordable taxicabs appeared—31 in all. For a fare of 5 mil-réis one could take a small tour of the downtown area. They would park before the Café Jeremias, on avenida Central. (Meneses 1966: 232–33)

Thus, while the cinematograph made familiar the sight of mechanical reproduction of movement, the popularization of motor cars automated, by means of mechanical transportation, a way of looking at the things around one as though they were pure images flashing by. Even as the movies seemed to make technical images even more verisimilar, the stream of autos, streetcars, and trains gave everyday objects a half-magical aura: it suddenly made them unreal. This is the topic of a novella by Júlia Lopes de Almeida, "O dedo do velho," included in the volume *A isca* (1923). The text opens with the protagonist in movement: "The automobile raced at top speed. Feeling the wind on his face, Claudino felt free of his worrisome thoughts" (Almeida 1923: 223). From within the car he had the impression that people were phantoms; the street seemed strange, the city itself was somehow unrecognizable:

At times it appeared to him that if he were to get out of the automobile and touch those people, even if only with the tips of his fingers, they would crumble into dust, like certain dead trees, corroded by worms. (Pp. 241–42)

The familiar sights around him become unreal, and inside the car Claudino, in an imperceptible torpor, partly loses the notion of time, as well as the feel of the places he is passing and of his destination. Thus he is surprised when his chauffeur asks him: "Did you say rua do Uruguai, sir?" And he does no more than reply: "Yes, rua do Uruguai" (p. 242).

Seeing the world pass by from inside a car, then, confirmed in everyday terms the changes that the popularization of the photographic camera and the cinematograph encouraged in the forms of perception. So it was that the name of one of the most popular illustrated magazines of the first few decades of the century was an onomatopoeic rendering of the sound of a car horn: *Fon-Fon*. It was advertised in 1907 as "a gay, political, critical, lively weekly. Damaged news. Wireless telegraph. Epidemic *crônicas*. Circulation: 100,000 kilometers an hour" (pp. 233–34).

But if automobiles were "delightful" for the way they shortened distances, as João do Rio stated in his *crônica* "A pressa de acabar" (The haste to get it over with), it had as a counterpart a "torment" with similar powers: the phonograph, thanks to which voices that were distant or even lost in time could be evoked.

The beginning of the systematic popularization of Edison phonographs in Brazil, in 1889, is a rather ironic affair, when one thinks of the new invention's ability to preserve what is lost. The talking machine had been shown in Rio de Janeiro for the first time in 1878 and 1879, first in "educational lectures" in a school, the Escola da Freguesia da Glória, then at a magician's establishment, F. Rodde's "Ao Grande Mágico," at rua do Ouvidor, 151, where an admission fee was charged. But it was only in 1889, when Carlos Monteiro de Sousa became Edison's representative in Brazil, that the phonograph began to be widely publicized. And the audience of the first three exhibitions of phonographs with removable cylinders was the imperial family.

What is ironic about this incident is that it took place on the eve of the proclamation of the republic, and that in its earliest use in Brazil the phonograph should have preserved the last voices of the empire—including that of the emperor himself.

The first demonstration took place on November 9, 1889. The operation of the device was explained, and recordings were played of the voices of "the visconde de Cavalcante, the comte de Villeneuve, Dr. Charcot the physician, M. Courdelet, the barão de Marajó, Senator Pereira da Silva, Marshall Âncora, Mr. Pinheiro Chagas, and the new ministers in Paris and London, respectively the barão de Penedo and the visconde de Arinos" (Franceschi 1984: 20). Also heard were two piano pieces, some cornet solos, the Portuguese national anthem, and the duet from Bizet's *Les pêcheurs de perles*. Finally the voice of Dom Pedro II was recorded:

The emperor, who had observed all the experiments with the utmost attention, said he would like to make a recording too, and as soon as a cylinder was prepared he spoke a few words, to the effect that he was "most pleased with what I have witnessed." A few moments later, the phonograph repeated the words that had just been recorded quite clearly. (P. 20)

Three days later, the emperor's voice and a few musical programs were shown to Princess Isabel, the conde d'Eu, the barão de Ramiz Galvão, the barão and baronesa de Muritiba, the baronesa de Suruí, the daughters of the visconde da Penha, and the sculptor Rodolfo Bernardelli. New recordings were also made on that evening: Prince Augusto sol-faing, the prince of Grão-Pará speaking, and one of the daughters of the visconde da Penha singing an "Ave Maria." There was yet another phonograph exhibition before the imperial family—the most melancholy of all. This was on November 14, 1889—the night before the proclamation of the republic. Present were the playwright França Júnior, the engineer Paulo de Frontin, the writer Afonso Celso, the barão de Maria Monteiro, the visconde de Taunay (a noted writer), and the conselheiro Catrambi.

Thus, from a political point of view the phonograph played the part of recording the voices of the rulers of the empire just before their fall from power. These recordings had a somewhat ambiguous effect: at the same time that they preserved and reproduced the voices, they also seemed to divest them of their earlier aura, in a rather cruel way. The voice of the emperor, recorded on November 9, was the voice of a deposed monarch only one week later. It was as though the daguerreotypes and phonograms that held such a fascination for Pedro II were announcing, without his being aware of the fact, the fading of the empire's insignia and the extinction of the monarchy. And the new devices, having been blessed by the emperor, were soon in the service of those who succeeded him in power.

An example of such later political use of technical reproduction is the omnipresence of portraits of President Floriano Peixoto, mentioned in Vaz's O professor Jeremias. In the novel, the narrator recalls that, when he was young, a portrait of the military president had been proudly exhibited in his father's house after the naval rebellion was crushed by Peixoto, right beside a portrait of his grandfather and an oval mirror in a gilt frame. "That portrait of the marshall in the living room, who received, according to its inscription, 'the tribute of the people of Sao Paulo,' was a symbol during my childhood," says Jeremias. "In it I saw and revered the man who stood for all the victories of Order against Anarchy, Democracy against Absolutism, Stability against Dissolution" (Vaz 1920: 39).

This powerful symbolic effect seems to result from the popularization of the industrial novelties and modern apparatuses that the emperor admired so much in the first few years of the republic. In the case of the phonograph, its dissemination picked up speed in 1891, when Frederico Figner become responsible for exhibiting the device around the country.

It seems that, at least for a while, the machine remained faithful to the empire. For Figner's first recordings, made in August 1891, in Belém, were a few words from the owner of the Hotel Central and "an impromptu speech against the republic made by Mr. Joaquim Cabral, a local lawyer" (Franceschi 1984: 17). About this speech, the Porto Alegre *Gazeta Americana* commented on December 17, 1892:

Figner also treats us to a rigmarole from a most gifted young man who has "Napoleon's army crossing the Red Sea, with Jericho ahead of him, and finding Jesus Christ heading an opposition newspaper," and other such characters that can only evoke a hearty peal of laughter. (Franceschi 1984: 17)

The criticism is aimed largely at monarchism, and only secondarily at the rhetoric of the young lawyer from Belém. For, contrary to what might be expected, the presence of the recording machine in no way contained the flowery oratory of the period. It was easy to laugh at a young provincial lawyer, but not at the bombast of those then seen as masters.

Rigmaroles, flights of rhetoric, music, voices—what was actually recorded mattered little; what counted was the spectacle of the new machine. It was like the early responses to the cinematograph. Here is an advertisement for a phonograph exhibition in Rio de Janeiro:

In this city, at rua do Ouvidor, 135, there will be an exhibition of *The talking machine*, the latest invention, and the most perfect, of the illustrious Edison. A good opportunity to get to know one of the strangest and most surprising inventions. This machine reproduces not only the human voice but also all sorts of sounds, such as songs, operas, and military marches. (Tinhorão 1981: 18)

The entrance fee was one mil-réis; the "shows" usually began at noon and ended at six. Audiences were quite large. In Belém, for instance, four thousand people paid to see and hear the new invention. The exhibitions met with the same success when Figner—or others, such as Manuel Ponte or Zé da Luz, who had fought in the Canudos rebellion—took it to Juiz de Fora, Ouro Preto, Paraíba, Natal, Salvador, Recife, or the federal capital.

By then "Figner was a millionaire: he had 37,000 mil-réis in the bank, after all expenses were paid, besides what he had sent to his father," writes

Franceschi. "For us today, what is significant about this is the fact that 50,000 people, in less than a year, had paid to go into a room and hear a phonograph" (Franceschi 1984: 21).

Such was the popularity of talking machines that on August 25, 1899, the enterprising Figner created the gramophone clubs, in partnership with Bernard Wilson Shaw. Each club was to have one hundred members, who would pay five mil-réis every week to take part in a weekly drawing for:

a model L Columbia gramophone for voice transmission, a small horn, a double rubber tube for the ear, and a box with 6 printed cylinders to be selected by the subscriber when he or she won the drawing or paid the fiftieth weekly install-ment. (Franceschi 1984: 28)

The clubs were also a success; soon there were twenty-seven in Rio. By then Figner was already selling phonographs, cylinders, and embossed tinfoil sheets. He wrote in his diary: "The more recordings are made, the more are sold" (Franceschi 1984: 35). Phonograms were much more affordable by 1908: according to Tinhorão, the "Sociedade Phonograph-ica Brasileira" advertised "gramophones at the reach of the poor and the rich, for 25, 40, 50, 60, 70, and 75 mil-réis" (Tinhorão 1981: 19). And Figner was a cautious businessman:

To make sure that the market would expand, since sales of cylinders depended on the increase in sales of phonographs, Frederico Figner was quick to set up a network of retailers and distributors. Thus in a few years the Bazar Edison had opened in Santos (rua General Câmara, 7) and had branches in Bahia and Pará; later distribution to Paraná and southern Minas Gerais was in the charge of Casa Murano, in São Paulo (rua Marechal Deodoro, 32). (Tinhorão 1981: 21)

The success of mechanical processes of sound recording and repro-duction in Brazil—to which the introduction of the gramophone in 1904 was to contribute—is indicated by the appearance of a monthly publica-tion, in 1902, dedicated to "phonographic art": *Echo Phonographico*. The magazine, which survived for two years, had a circulation of twelve thou-sand, a significant figure if the number of potential consumers at the time is considered. The magazine's success is not surprising when one takes into account the growing number of owners of phonographs and gram-ophones, as well as the fact that Figner's record company, International Talking Machine, sold 840,000 records between 1911 and 1912 alone. Franceschi comments that "the market tended to grow with every passing year." As an example, he notes that "two or three years later 280,000 copies were sold of the song 'A baratinha' " (Franceschi 1984: 93).

From the literary point of view, at least one consequence was to be expected: the concern with reproducing oral forms of expression should decline, since sound recording was able to preserve regional dialects, lawyers' flights of rhetoric, and everyday speech with equal faithfulness. Perhaps that is why Godofredo Rangel, in his sensitive depiction of provincial life in *Vida ociosa*, felt the need to describe a broken-down gramophone. It is as if he wanted to suggest that his novel did not intend to reproduce "mechanically" the speech of country folk or anything of the sort, but instead to present possible forms of perceiving time or telling stories other than those that were dominant at the time. Instead of reproducing scenes of provincial life, his idea was to emphasize the figure of the narrator.

The diffusion of sound recording in Brazil may also have reinforced the preference for preciosity in vocabulary and tortuous syntax in part of the work of Coelho Neto and in Bilac's poetry, to name only two of the writers of the time. For the laughter that greeted Figner's recording of a speech by a Belém lawyer in 1892 apparently had little impact on the Brazilian taste for eloquence. In an interview given to *O Jornal* in 1927, Alcântara Machado lamented: "Here there is no prose, only oratory." He also expressed a hope: "Let prose be freed from rhetoric." In the early twentieth century, rhetorical ornamentation was one of the most common ways to mark the difference between the field of the "literary" or "artistic" and that of the technical processes of production and diffusion of images and voices. And whereas Rangel's project was to distinguish narration from mere repetition, the contrast between ornamentation and technical reproduction was that of much of Brazilian cultural production from the 1890's to the 1920's.

The taste for ornate façades was also present in the musical production of the period, as well as in the styles of musical interpretation. On this topic, Wisnik comments:

In Brazilian musical production of the period there is a genre akin to Coelho Neto's literary regionalism: the "characteristic piece." In the early twentieth century, one often finds hybrid specimens of "Brazilian music" as enclaves in suites and rhapsodies, syncopated motifs squeezed between piano trills and flourishes that were totally incompatible with the folk themes themselves. (Wisnik 1983: 28)

Thus music was treated as image: it was its function to describe major civic events, popular sentiments, and natural scenery. These romantic descriptions were infallibly accompanied by sentimentalism in the interpretation, according to Wisnik. This was one of the causes of the "piano-latry" that Mário de Andrade attacked in the magazine *Klaxon*: "Our music remains in the Romantic period; and Chopin is the sobbing ideal of all our piano-playing young ladies" (p. 76).

It is as though there was a silent discussion between musical interpretation and the new techniques of sound recording, the former attempting to affirm its difference from recorded concerts and pieces by underscoring the *presence* of the interpreter, overdramatizing the written music, overburdening it with ornamentation. Wisnik explains:

The problem is vexing to the extent that musical production fundamentally depends on the conditions of reproduction at the musician's disposal, particularly when one remembers that performance is closely akin to creation, and that the meaning of the work largely depends on the decisions the performer makes while playing. (Wisnik 1983: 30)

Thus, the obsession with virtuosity and with excessive sentimentality invests the most popular concerts of the 1910's and 1920's with a new meaning. The new meaning that derived from this interpretive technique was usually external to the work played, centering sometimes on the person of the soloist or the conductor, sometimes on the piece's "patriotic" intentions. This brought about a nearly insurmountable incompatibility between the obsession with musical description and virtuosity on the one hand, and the character of modern musical production on the other. Similarly, picturesque regionalism, decorative use of unusual, archaic, and scientific vocabulary, and a fetishistic attitude toward ornamentation were in sharp contrast to a no-frills sort of literature, the earliest, isolated examples of which appeared in the 1900's, and which came into its own through some authors of the 1920's.

Sandwich Men

An anecdote involving Aluísio Azevedo and the publication of his novel *O homem*, as recalled by Coelho Neto, may serve as a convenient point of departure for understanding the rise of the advertising industry in Brazil. In 1887 in a Rio restaurant, Azevedo—so the story runs—stuck a label announcing *O homem* on a bun; when a patron found it and complained about the restaurant's unsanitary ways, he explained that the label had to do with a 300-page novel published by Garnier that was to go on sale two days later (Machado Neto 1973: 185). According to Coelho Neto, Azevedo then offered a somewhat backhanded defense of advertising:

I'll wind up pushing a cart up and down the streets yet, like a man selling pineapples or watermelons, advertising my novels in loud cries. What good is imagination, or style? What really counts is publicity. If the author is silent, no matter how eloquent his books may be, they will sit in the back of the bookstore until they are sold by the kilogram for wrapping paper. (P. 186)

If the story is to be believed, at least in part, then Aluísio Azevedo wholeheartedly embraced publicity as a necessity for a professional writer. Not only that, he also understood the need to incorporate consciously into his book the expectations of his potential public. This would explain his adoption of naturalist models. The immediate response should then be increased sales.

Only one year later, however, another writer, Raul Pompéia, expressed in his novel O Ateneu (1888) a categorical refusal of advertising of any kind. He particularly ruled out the adoption of a journalistic sort of prose in order to popularize the reading of fiction. In opposition to advertising, Pompéia proposes memory and a strictly private world as the basic sources of literary creation. Thus O Ateneu may be thought of as a novel that, written in a period of burgeoning modernization in Brazil, when the dialogue between literature and technology was becoming more intense, opts for a unique and somewhat archaeological path: the affirmation of subjectivity and of the narrator at a time when the narrator's survival was beginning to be seen as endangered.

O Ateneu may thus be construed as a duel between the sandwich man and the man of letters. Their weapons are advertising and memory respectively. On one side, a narrator remembers and founds his narrative on the reconstruction of his own experience: "Some remembered sounds remain forever, like echoes of the past. Sometimes I remember the piano, and then that particular day is brought back to me" (Pompéia 1976: 199); a chain of impressions re-creates Serginho's adolescence archaeologically. On the other side, we have a character who is a sort of sandwich man: "The advertisement merged with him, suppressed him, replaced him, and he rejoiced, like a poster glorying in its own redness" (p. 70): this is a description of Aristarco, proprietor of the school where Serginho studies. On one side, "a succession of mental pictures";[3] on the other, a "static photograph" (p. 30). Thus it is in opposition to Aristarco that the character of the narrator is built. And the gradual destruction of this "genius of publicity" is precisely the subject of Pompéia's "nostalgic chronicle," which in this way attempts to delimit the field of literature, contrasting it with advertising and technically produced imagery.

Whether accepting advertising as inevitable or electing it as one's opponent, both Aluísio Azevedo and Raul Pompéia point to the growth of advertising in the late 1880's, a visible consequence of the advent of new techniques of mechanical printing and reproduction.

It was only in the 1860's that posters, pamphlets, and painted panels began to be widely used to advertise products and commercial establishments in the major Brazilian cities. Until then, the small circulation of newspapers and the difficulty of printing in large numbers such things as pamphlets and directions of wonder drugs drastically restricted the items that could be advertised. Hats, mats, shoes, fabrics, sofas, crystals, mirrors, slaves, engravings, cuspidors, pianos, combs, snuff, ointments, books, schools: ads for such items were addressed to a public consisting of noblemen and rich families. At that time, properly speaking there was no commercial advertising.[4] In the first half of the nineteenth century in Brazil, advertising was concentrated on what was exceptional.

Those early ads spoke of curious, unique products, of unusual forms of entertainment, such as the presence of a magician or some foreign opera company. Some were personal messages, with almost the character of private correspondence. Here is an ad published in *Diário de Pernambuco* on August 2, 1844:

The gentleman who keeps stealing pigeons . . . is requested to let them go, otherwise his name will be published, and the law will be relied on to recover the large number of pigeons he has caught . . . and also his manner of life and the goings-on on the second floor will be made known; all of this will be done unless the pigeons are returned. (Freyre 1979: 15)

Here is another example of highly personalized advertising, published on September 23, 1830:

A slave woman is on sale for such a low price that it will seem incredible to acquire one for so little at such a time as now; the said slave woman has no vices and is a skilled baker and her only disadvantage are her unpleasant looks, which is why she is being sold. (P. 15)

The tone is so intimate that it is as though the advertiser could name those he was addressing if requested to do so. But this situation changed dramatically with the advent of printed advertisements, companies specializing in publicity, and the first professionals in advertising. Now the text was no longer composed by the person interested in placing the ad; nor could the new public—the readers of newspapers, pamphlets, and posters—be addressed in a highly personal tone. The advertising industry had begun to take shape.

Ramos (1985) suggests that among the earliest representatives of early modern advertising are Henrique Fleiuss's poster for the magazine *Semana Ilustrada* (1860); the first illustrated ads published on the last pages of *Mequetrefe* and *O Mosquito* (1875), some of them drawn by the novelist Aluísio Azevedo during his stint as a caricaturist; the simultaneous publication of seven ads by Julião Machado, each of a different size and with its own text and illustrations, in *A Bruxa* (May 1896); and the appearance of the trimonthly *O Mercúrio* (1898), originally projected to specialize in illustrated advertising. Another significant fact, according to Ramos (p. 19), is the creation of small magazines, such as *Vida Paulista* (1903) and *Arara* (1904), "published in São Paulo for years, supported by local advertisers"; these magazines are evidence of "the existence of an advertising business with a fledgling organization, centered on the role of the advertising canvasser."

By the 1910's and 1920's, there was good money to be made in canvassing. Witness the case of Ernest von Ockel and his Empresa Distribuidora de Anúncios Nacionais e Estrangeiros:

> In 1913 or 1914, a young German nobleman came to São Paulo from the port of Santos with his family, banished for political reasons; so it was that Baron Ernest von Ockel was forced to come to Brazil. At about the age of 20, young von Ockel opened a small firm in São Paulo called Empresa Distribuidora de Anúncios [Advertisement Distribution Company] that received advertisements of all kinds from a number of places, including Germany—where he now had not only friends but also commercial partners—and placed them in local magazines and newspapers. The small firm grew, and its name likewise was extended to Empresa Distribuidora de Anúncios Nacionais e Estrangeiros [in Brazil and Abroad]. (Lima 1985: 38–39)

This name was later simplified to EDANEE—Empresa de Publicidade e Livraria (Advertising Company and Book Store), where von Ockel worked originally with "a single small Minerva press in which he printed advertisements and then sent the proofs to newspapers" (p. 39). In 1928, his company grew with the opening of EDANEE's printing plant.

Advertising as a profession attracted not only enterprising immigrants and businessmen of various kinds, but also many of the best-known men of letters of the early twentieth century, who did not think twice before accepting the role of sandwich man. Bilac, Emílio de Meneses, Hermes Fontes, and Bastos Tigre are only a few of the writers who were actively engaged in writing advertising copy in the form of quatrains and sonnets.

The case of Bastos Tigre is particularly significant; advertising provided most of his income. Eventually he opened a firm—Publicidade Bastos Tigre—that advertised such diverse products as Confeitaria Colombo (a café), Cafiaspirina Bayer (a brand of aspirin), Cigarros York (cigarettes), Magazine Notre Dame (a department store), Drogaria V. Silva (a pharmacy), and Cerveja Fidalga (a beer). Some of his slogans are well known in Brazil to this day (see Meneses 1966): "If it's Bayer, it's the best" (for Bayer aspirin), "All roads lead to the Roma" (Roma restaurant), "The quality is aristocratic, the price is plebeian" (Fidalga beer), "Medicine in the bottle, health in your body" (Peitoral Infantil cough syrup). Even more famous—many Brazilians know it by heart to this day—is the stanza he wrote for the patent medicine Rhum Creosotado: "Please regard, gentle passenger, / The gorgeous young beauty / Who is sitting by your side. / Incredible as it may seem, / She nearly died of bronchitis: / Rhum Creosotado saved her life."

Tigre also wrote the "Bromilíadas," a parody of *The Lusiads* published weekly, in two-stanza installments, on the last page of the magazine *D. Quixote*, as advertising for Bromil cough syrup. Tigre's idea was to show off his technical expertise as a poet as a way of ennobling the product he was advertising. This is why the sonnet was his preferred form in ads; the familiar form and the polish of the verse were expected to heighten the value of the products being sold.

Other fine examples of this strategy are "Um milagre" (A miracle), published by Emílio de Meneses in *D. Quixote* in 1917, also as an advertisement for Bromil, and the curious sonnet "Fantasia de bonde" (A streetcar daydream), an advertisement for Pilogênio hair tonic, by Bastos Tigre:

> Thursday, nine-thirty, on the Jockey Club
> Streetcar. On the seat next to my own
> Sits a buxom young lady, rather pretty,
> In a white dress with embroidered filet lace.
>
> She seems oblivious to the world around her
> And fails to notice that I fix my gaze
> On the down that her upper lip does darken,
> Well-nigh a mustache, if the truth be told.

A likely explanation springs to mind:
She loved somebody, loved with all her heart;
This someone left her; she, with grief distraught,

Her own life would have taken, had she not
Instead of poison—by mistake or what?—
Pressed to her lips a vial of Pilogênio.

But quatrains were the most popular form—rhymed, strongly ca-denced lines that were easily memorized. Here is an ad for Andalusa coffee by Bastos Tigre: "Set yourself a course in life / That will lead you to success. / Every morning, as you rise, / Drink a cup of Andalusa." Here is one for Casa Muniz: "Good old Casa Muniz / Is as happy as can be. / In glass, china, or crystals / It need fear no rivalry."

Let us examine three examples by Bilac. The first, for a patriotically named Brazilian candle factory, has all the ingredients typical of Bilac's serious poetry—the jingoistic tone, the exclamations, the apostrophes: "Vanquished, to darkest oblivion / Is foreign industry reduced. / O Fa-therland, proudly exult / Over 'Brasileira' candles." The very heavens proclaim the excellence of Cruzeiro (Southern Cross) matches in the second example: " 'Tis All Hallows Day! / The Master of the Revels decrees / That throughout the sky shall burn / 'Cruzeiro' matches all around." Last, here is Bilac's ad for Brilhante matches, for which he was paid the princely sum of 100 mil-réis: "Hear me all that smokers be: / Both the noble Prince of Wales / And President Campos Sales / Use none but Brilhante matches" (Pontes 1944, 2: 402).

There were so many famous writers writing advertising copy that in 1913 the Benz, Steinberg, Meyer & Co. automobile company used the figure of a member of the Brazilian Academy of Letters making a speech in an ad published in *Fon-Fon* magazine. A portly gentleman in academic dress stands behind a table on which there is a sheaf of papers and a glass of water. In his left hand he holds a miniature Benz car. The caption ad reads:

MAY I HAVE YOUR ATTENTION PLEASE ...
I would like to say, gentlemen, that reports concerning the political cam-paigning I supposedly have been indulging in are vastly exaggerated. However, I make no bones about speaking out for
BENZ AUTOMOBILES,
which indeed, for their *resistance*, for their *elegance*, deserve to be praised by men like me.
(The speaker is enthusiastically applauded.)[5]

The man's face bears a striking resemblance to that of the historian Oliveira Lima, a prominent member of the academy at the time. This ad calls attention to the fact that many writers at the time were working as admen, a work that was handsomely paid—but that sometimes evoked feelings of guilt. One understands why Bilac should wax patriotic in a candle ad, or Bastos Tigre should display his versifying skills and emulate Camões in an epic campaign for a brand of cough syrup. Their intention, it seems, was to ennoble their work in advertisement by associating it with patriotism and elevated literary genres.

Emílio de Meneses, in contrast, seemed to laugh at his own stints as literary sandwich man and signed many of his ads in verse "Gabriel d'Anúncio"—a pun on Gabriele D'Annunzio and *anúncio*, Portuguese for "advertisement." He makes no attempt to ennoble his hack work. Here is an ad he wrote for Brahma beer, published on the anniversary of the death of Joaquim Manuel de Macedo, April 11: "On this date Macedo died, who wrote / "The blond youth," and "The little brunette" too. / When I reread him, these are my secret thoughts: / O for some golden lager and some rich dark porter!" (Meneses 1980: 196). Rather than poeticize his copy, Meneses does precisely the opposite: he puns on the names of two novels by Macedo (*O moço loiro* and *A moreninha*). Perhaps unconsciously, he also highlights the redefinition of the idea of art that was taking place in the period, which included a widening of the range of materials seen as fit for literary treatment—side by side with classical forms and images and ill-lit interiors, restaurants, department stores, cough syrup, and beer.

But it was not only by providing work for writers that the advertising industry affected the Brazilian literary system. Books also began to be seen as merchandise that could be advertised. At first this was done by listing "Works on sale" inconspicuously among ads of various sorts. "Whenever books were advertised, it was in the form of brief announcements to the effect that a certain book was 'forthcoming,' or 'soon on sale,' or 'just released,'" writes Lima (1985: 61). Another kind of book ad, just as unappealing, "was aimed at a specific public: 'editions for children,' 'for young people,' 'for teachers'; there were also somewhat more laudatory ads that said books were 'the best friends' or made 'the best gifts'" (p. 61). Fiorentino adds that there were ads for "books for parties and school prizes," "books of lucky incantations," "books that should be read by young ladies" (1982: 18).

But some were able to use advertising more effectively. Monteiro Lobato wrote of his first book for children, in May 1921: "My *Narizinho*, of which I printed 50,500 copies—the biggest edition in the world!—has to be forced down the public's throats, like a mother giving her children castor oil. I spent 4,000 mil-réis on a full-page ad in a local newspaper" (Fiorentino 1982: 18). Lobato was concerned not only with advertising but also with distribution and graphic design. He hired Antônio Vieira Paim, Benedito Bastos Belmonte, and Mick Carnicelli to design covers, illustrations, and other graphic features of books. Lobato reminisced in 1941: "I hired draftsmen, ordered loud colors for the covers. And illustrations too!"[6]

To make his books more salable, Lobato often altered the division of the chapters or even changed the original title. He allegedly told an author to "give it a woman's name if possible, for prurient readers will buy it if they smell a woman somewhere; it takes commercial psychology to be a publisher" (Hallewell 1985: 251). To his friend Godofredo Rangel he gave different suggestions. For instance, in a letter dated February 8, 1919, Lobato wrote:

Vida ociosa has arrived. I would advise you to replace the chapter numbers, which are uncommercial, with chapter names, which are extremely commercial. To me, a novel with numbered chapters is terribly arid. And one with a tempting title in each chapter seems fertile. (Lobato 1968, 1: 189)

From the commercial angle, Lobato's suggestion apparently had the expected result. "In early 1920, the company sold an average four thousand books a month; in 1921, a new edition was sold out every week," writes Hallewell (1985: 253).

Advertising, in addition to influencing sales, became a literary subject. The topic is the object of bitter reflections by two friends who study the ads in the newspaper—houses for rent, fortune tellers, and the like—in "Anúncios ... Anúncios ... ," a *crônica* by Lima Barreto included in *Feiras e mafuás*. It is treated in a lighter, more ironic tone by João do Rio in *A alma encantadora das ruas* (1910), where the author describes the various forms of street advertising:

One fine day, the street proclaims an excellent truth: that words are carried by the wind. So, in fear, we create the sandwich man, the walking poster; while he sleeps, we stick posters onto his board, with plenty of glue and ingenuity, proclaiming the best preserves, the sternest wine, the tastiest sweetmeat, the most generous political ideal, not only in printed letters but also in allegorical pictures, to spare him the trouble of reading, to cherish his ignorance, to make it merrier. (Rio 1910: 27)

So, as if printed ads were not enough, advertising took to the streets—posters, sandwich men, throwaways, signboards, movie-theater curtains covered with commercial announcements. The façades themselves may be seen as advertisements for the modernization that the largest Brazilian cities were then going through; in this period there was a veritable obsession with façades, which became the dominant element in buildings. And, of course, there is also another sense of "façade" relevant here—the concern with elegant clothes and display was associated with the growth of advertising. Martins Fontes exulted:

Oh! the toilettes of the admirable caricaturist, Calixto Cordeiro! Lovely! Lovely! Fantastic! Fantastic!

Oh! the large hats of Emílio [de Meneses], natural children of a top hat and a derby!—Guima's [Guimarães Passos's] spats, in all colors, imported straight from London.[7]

The word is *display, publicize*. Everything must be exhibited: from the city itself, constantly depicted in albums of views, postcards, panoramas, magazines, down to the human figure itself, which served as the medium for displaying fashion.

Thus it makes perfect sense that Toledo Malta should have chosen the name of a brand of champagne for the protagonist of his novel *Madame Pommery*. Or that a poster should be able to inspire amorous feelings, as in an "Intermezzo" in José Agudo's *Gente rica* (1912):[8]

Leivas . . . noticed that the scaffolding of the new Rotisserie Sportsman was covered with posters filled with huge multicolored letters, and the name that was most prominent in them was Mina Lanzi—Mina Lanzi in red, in blue, in green—and in each poster the photograph of the famous actress shone; sometimes only her head and torso were shown, while in others she appeared in various positions, as each of the various characters she had played on the stage.

Ah! the suggestive power of advertisements!

Particularly when this power is exerted on the mind of one who is idle and has a goodly supply of bills in one's wallet! (Agudo 1912: 128–29)

Just as Madame Pommery is a brand name, Leivas is suddenly gripped by passion for a product; for he is not interested in Mina Lanzi the person but in the photographs, the posters with her likeness that are all over the city.

In Léo Vaz's novel *O professor Jeremias*, brand names and labels set off a chain of memories. As he gazes at the shelves in the pharmacy, on which a bottle bearing a certain "favorite label" is kept, Jeremias is suddenly transported to another time, a different pharmacy, and other printed figures:

I looked at the label and heard the figures speak, and was reminded of my Pirassaguera days, when I used to frequent a different pharmacy, the one kept by the old German Niemayer, to ask him for Bristol almanacs, which carried the stories of GUILHERME, THE LION, AND THE VELOCIPEDE, IN 6 PANELS. (Vaz 1920: 174)

"All we have to do is raise our heads, and the signboards will tell the story of our lives," writes Rio (1910). They also tell us how in Brazil, from the 1880's to the 1920's, advertising gradually became an important element in Brazilian cultural life. It generated a brand of intellectual whose professionalization was associated with his work as advertising man. It directly influenced the increase in the potential public for literature. And it seemed organically connected to the passion for ornamentation, for façades, that characterized Brazil at the time.

The influence of advertising may even suggest a peculiar view of literature. This much seems to be implied by the graphic design of a book like Paulo Mendes de Almeida's *Cartazes* (Signboards, 1928). The cover, by Arnaldo Barbosa, attempted to represent the proliferation of street ads— for Guaraná Espumante, Lacta, Para-Todos, Sudam, Leiteria Campo-Bello—and the book began with the following explanation: "Advertisements on the cover of a book of poetry! ... What's so terrible about that? After all, what are published poems if not advertisements for emotions experienced? Signboards, signboards ... " (Lima 1985: 153). This example, at least, is one of wholehearted approval of a reconciliation between literature and advertising.

A similar development is the rise of a curious genre of movie, a mixture of fiction and advertising, in the early history of the movie industry in São Paulo:[9] films like *Um roubo da Casa Michel* (A theft at Casa Michel) and *24 horas na vida de uma mulher elegante* (Twenty-four hours in the life of an elegant woman), which included advertisements for the commercial establishments that financed their production. And just as Bilac, Meneses, and Tigre were in the sphere of literature, Antônio Campos and Gilberto Rossi, in the first years of Paulista movies, were inevitably drawn into working for the infant advertising industry in their struggle for professionalization.

In the case of men of letters, however, the sort of endorsement of advertising expressed in *Cartazes* is something of an exception; irony was by far the more typical response. An example is given by the bogus ad published in number 7 of the modernist magazine *Klaxon*, for a "sonnet, madrigal, ballad, and quatrain factory" named Pannosopho, Pateromnium & Co. A price list was included: "Quatrains, 0.20 to 1 mil-réis. Ballads, from 1.30 to 5 mil-réis"; sonnets were offered at different prices, depending on the model chosen: "simple, rhymed, with alliterations, or with punch lines" (Lima 1985: 72). In the following issue of *Klaxon*, Pannosopho, Pateromnium & Co. ran another ad: "In response to a large demand, we have decided to open in the city of São Paulo a Laboratory of Chemical-Grammatical Analyses, in addition to a modern Office of Literary Investigation and Arrest" (p. 72).

But this gag must be seen in light of the fact that by then it was possible to look at the old sandwich men from a distance. The situation was different for those who actually experienced the clash between sonnets and cough syrups, the time when book titles and chapter headings began to be chosen on grounds of salability. When one thinks of the division within the work of Bilac, the irony of Toledo Malta's brand-name heroine, the resort to memory as a point of departure for writing in Raul Pompéia and Joaquim Nabuco, the antiquarian prose of Godofredo Rangel or Afonso Arinos, the poetry of interiors of the penumbristas,[10] one realizes that the dialogue between literature and publicity in the three-decade period beginning at the turn of century was less a dialogue than a tense encounter. The tension was made even stronger when a third interlocutor was introduced, a close relative of advertising, closely connected to it: the press. I now examine this connection.

Under Pressure

"To pay one's rent with articles—now, isn't that simply wonderful?" (Lobato 1968, 1: 273) Lobato wrote in 1909, when the *Tribuna de Santos* paid him forty mil-réis for a series of articles, which allowed him to pay two months' rent. "As I write these words, the typographer casts his sweaty, urgent eye on them," Pedro Kilkerry commented in his *crônica* of March 4, 1913, for *Jornal Moderno*. "I sentence you to write for the papers for the rest of your days, whether or not you have anything to say, whether or not you are sick, whether or not you have any desire to write!" says the devil to the writer in a *crônica* published by Bilac in *Gazeta de Notícias* in 1897.

The passage by Lobato is the expression of unmitigated joy for the professionalization of writers, which was then beginning. Kilkerry's observation expresses, with no guilt, the closer relationship between writers and the press, which implied the need to write under pressure—pressure not only from the new media, but also from a scarcely avoidable awareness of the corrosion of time, of "chronometers that measure only seconds of ambition, brand-new sensations," of knowing one is writing "within time, in the waves of time," "where everything is something else or tends toward something else" (Campos 1985: 166–67). In Bilac's text, the idea of the devil imposing on the writer the task of writing *crônicas* points to a view of journalism that combines bad conscience and fatalism.

Though their perspectives are different, the three writers seem to point in the same direction: the prevailing form of production and diffusion of literature in the period; its direct connection with the new commercial press, which was then becoming consolidated and offered men of letters the possibility of professionalization, through journalism.

From a strictly technical angle, the transformation that took place in the Brazilian press at the turn of the century was the use of photochemical methods of reproduction. The turning point was May 1, 1900, the day on which Alvaro de Teffé launched *Revista da Semana*. Until then, the most commonly adopted methods of reproduction were lithography—which meant that the cartoonist Angelo Agostini had to draw "directly on the surface of a heavy stone, in negative fashion, so that the printed result would look natural"[11]—and engraving on zinc or copper—which required drawing on gelatin-coated paper, "in the exact size of the reproduction to be made, however small" (Lima 1969: 138). Beginning in 1900, these methods were replaced by photozincography and photoengraving.

Another significant change was "the publication of color illustrations on glossy paper, in rotary presses" (Lima 1968: 141). The practice was first adopted by the *Gazeta de Notícias* on July 7, 1907. On Sundays, the newspaper published "cartoons using the three-color process, with the help of foreign artists—the painter Apolo Pauny and the lithographer Júlio Raison. The high point of this period was the publication of Calixto's great satires on the Hermes da Fonseca administration" (Sodré 1983: 300–301).

Together with these technical improvements, the circulation of publications increased, the number of pages grew, distribution became more efficient, production costs were cut, and graphic design improved. At the turn of the century, newspapers became middle-sized industrial establishments. Writes Sodré (p. 275): "Small newspapers with a simple structure gave way to news companies, with a specific structure and specialized machinery." The industrialization of the press made newspapers reach out for a mass public, which in early-twentieth-century Brazil was something of a problem, not least because only a minority of the population was literate: in 1890, 18.5 percent of the total (11,444,891); in 1900, 33.1 percent of the total (13,422,259).[12] These figures provide the background for statements such as that by Samuel Oliveira suggesting that the circulation of newspapers, though larger than that of books, was far from satisfactory: "Not even newspapers have reasonable circulations; if you add up those of all the papers published in this national capital where one million people live, you will get less than 50,000 copies" (Sevcenko 1983: 89). Bilac made a similar complaint in a letter to João do Rio, though he conceded that newspapers provided writers with one of their few opportunities to reach a wider audience:

Newspapers pose a complicated problem. They give us a chance to speak to a certain number of people who would not know us if they did not read the daily paper; to newspaper owners, the lack of education of readers is a factor that limits the circulation of their papers. All Rio dailies together sell fewer than 150 copies a day, an insignificant figure for any second-rate European paper. And there are eight papers here! This shows that the public doesn't read. (Rio n.d.: 89)

In addition to attracting readers to literary texts, journalistic work at the time offered writers their only possibility of professionalization. Other possible sources of income were a government job, a teaching position, the diplomatic service, work in specific campaigns—for instance, for literacy education, compulsory military service, elementary education, or Brazil's entry in World War I—writing textbooks and other books for children, or lecturing. And if men like Tigre and, more sporadically, Bilac and Meneses, earned money from advertising or occasionally writing subtitles for films, journalism provided a steady income for most men of letters in turn-of-the-century Brazil.

As Miceli notes, "Intellectual life was entirely dominated by the major papers, which were the main outlet for cultural production and the main source of paid positions for intellectuals" (1977: 15). Broca observes that regular salaries and payments per contribution had become quite reasonable by then: "The *Jornal do Commercio* paid from 30 to 60 mil-réis per article; the *Correio da Manhã* paid 50" (1960: 216). In 1907 the *Gazeta de Notícias* was paying a regular monthly salary to Bilac, *O País* to Medeiros e Albuquerque, and the *Correio da Manhã* to Coelho Neto. On September 1, 1907, "*Gazeta de Notícias* boasted, with some exaggeration, that it paid its contributors in Rio more than Paris newspapers paid, and that the newspaper did so as a sign of respect for men of letters, for not even a daily article signed by the nation's most celebrated writer had any effect on the paper's circulation" (p. 216). In 1906, Alphonsus de Guimaraens was being paid 400 mil-réis by the São Paulo *Gazeta*; by 1915, Humberto de Campos was making 300 mil-réis a month, and his salary rose to 500 in 1928. Such handsome salaries were not exactly the rule—for instance, the *Jornal do Commercio* paid Constâncio Alves 50 mil-réis for his *crônicas* for at least thirty-six years (see Machado Neto 1973: 81)—but nevertheless there was a clear economic link between literary production and journalism. On this, Miceli comments:

What had been a "tolerated" practice for some of the Romantics (such as Alencar and Macedo), and for some members of the generation of 1870 (such as Machado de Assis) had become a regular activity providing an increasingly indispensable additional income, was now the central activity of the "Anatolians" [followers of Anatole France]. (Miceli 1977: 72)

What made journalism central to them was not only the fact that it made possible a certain degree of professionalization but also the prestige and political influence it seemed to confer on men of letters. Thus, Miceli observes, "The post of editorialist was highly desirable, and for many writers it became the first step in a political career" (p. 73). For as a consequence of the process of modernization undergone by Brazilian newspapers in the beginning of the century, the kind of work available to writers was less and less "literary." Rather than produce stories and poems, they were expected to write reports and interviews; instead of polishing *crônicas*, they edited copy. "Many writers began handling crime news and writing unsigned notices, in addition to the by-lined articles that were sometimes published on the front page" (Broca 1960: 220).

This change was duly noted at the very moment it was taking place by one of these journalist-literati: Coelho Neto. Here is a part of his dialogue with João do Rio, originally published in 1905:

"Let us then talk of journalism, since we must. In Brazil, journalism had always been political. When the public grew weary, the political fad was replaced by industrial processes. Newspapers were no longer ballot boxes, but rather ... "
"What?"
"Workshops. This has been mostly good for our literature. Since the papers never dared to educate, now they accept a piece not on account of the author's genius, but in function of the public's taste. Sometimes they are perverse." (Rio 1922: 61)

Coelho Neto seems to foresee that industrialization implied a tendency to standardize the language of editors and contributors. He writes: "As to the literature we publish in the papers, it is reminiscent of the books printed at the time of the Holy Office. It must bear the imprint not of the Inquisition, but of the editor-in-chief" (Rio 1922: 61). The importance of this observation is underscored by the fact that most of Coelho Neto's work was written for the papers. *Turbilhão*, *Capital Federal*, and *Rei fantasma* were not simply published as feuilletons: they were written as such, piecemeal, responding to reader's reactions and availability of space in the papers. "I work on a constant basis," he wrote to João do Rio. "Only my novellas were written and retouched before being dispatched to the publishers. All of my other works have been written for the papers on a day-to-day basis" (p. 56). Coelho Neto deals with the imperative of standardization mostly by using a tone and vocabulary that contrast with the simplification and the supposedly "objective" tone that are characteristic of journalistic writing.

It is as if the writer were drawing thick borders around his literary contributions. This way neither traditional literary forms nor conventional journalism is challenged; instead, a sort of signboard is put up on the façade, saying, in the most tortuous syntax, with a rich vocabulary and adjectives aplenty: This place is reserved for Literature. Like the ads in verse, this was a sort of advertising for poetic craftsmanship. "A few providential quotations did the trick of identifying the intellectual," notes Sevcenko (1983: 99). "As had occurred with literature, clichés and platitudes became the hallmark of the littérateur." Thus excessive ornamentation was one of the preferred forms of delimiting the space of "art," the space of the man of letters, in the newspaper. And in this way neither the privileged literary forms nor the standardization of texts imposed by journalistic work was questioned.

So it was that Bilac followed in Coelho Neto's footsteps in his relationship with the press, though occasionally he indulged in a mea culpa: "But if a young writer were to come to me, on this sad day, and ask my desolate, sad, autumnal being for advice," he confesses to João do Rio, "this is all I would tell him: Love your art above all things, and have the courage, which I did not have, to starve to death rather than prostitute your talents" (Rio n.d.: 11–12). The combination of bad conscience and fatalism that marked Bilac's attitude toward professionalization in journalism led him neither to a more consistent evaluation of the emerging newspaper organizations of his time nor to a reflection on the possibility of incorporating journalistic resources into his literary work, with the necessary changes. The most that he does is to include in his writings occasional gibes at news and ads published in newspapers, poke gentle fun at the press, and—a rather indirect reaction—adopt a pompous diction in his *crônicas*, in contrast with the colloquial tone of journalistic language.

Examples of Bilac's mild irony are his glosses on advertisements and news items. Here is one on an ad put up by a charwoman who claimed to be an expert at making beds: "Lady, won't you leave off / Making beds, it's no great matter! / For *un*making them with skill / Is a labor so much better!" On the news that triplets had been born in a local hospital: "Says the 'paper' (inter alia) / That a month ago some Eve / Bore, in the Misericórdia, / Three children all at once. / In a case like this what strikes me / As worthy of admiration / Is not Eve's great patience, / But Adam's consummate skill." On an obituary: "When he landed, stiff and hefty, / Upon Heaven's mighty scales, / St. Michael asked him, smiling: / 'Mind if I cheat, Manoel?' "[13]

Bilac's opposition to journalism is then just another subject for a *crônica*, to be treated with endearing irony and to generate a literary trifle. For to Bilac what distinguishes the language of the littérateur from the reporter's is a greater adroitness. Thus a writer like Bilac could use verse as a vehicle for news or *crônicas*, as in a text published in 1898, a part of which is transcribed below:

> Such days of flat prose!
> O God! for a break!
> Muse, may your fair hand
> See me through this week.
>
> Let the *crônica* flow on
> Through this Sunday sweet
> As a river with cool waters
> Across a boundless desert …
>
> Muse, let us metrify,
> And tell the population:
> "Thank heaven for verse
> To help our digestion … "
>
> For, O Muse, poesy is still
> Above all, par excellence,
> The manure that helps digest
> The substance of our existence.
>
> (Pontes 1944: 517–18)

As these stanzas indicate, Bilac had no intention of using poetry or ornamentation as resources for tightening the language of journalism or discussing the conception of news prevalent at the time. For men of letters, the problem seemed to be merely to stake out their space and label it their territory, thus justifying their presence in the realm of journalism. The sole difference between their approach and that of newsmen was that they provided a literary frame for the material they presented: "What when told in prose / May seem rough and bitter / Told in verse flows down one's throat / Smooth and sweet like honey ... " In his *crônicas* in verse, he sings of lack of money, currency devaluation, and other such matters, like any journalist—except that his lines scan and rhyme.

Thus the display of style becomes increasingly indispensable as a "technically conditioned language"[14] is progressively affirmed, writers settle into their role of newsmen, submitting to the "imprint . . . of the editor-in-chief" (to quote Coelho Neto again) to such an extent that even in their nonjournalistic texts telltale signs of the growing standardization of language begin to appear. It is at this point that writers feel compelled to fictionalize or address in a straightforward fashion the possibility of affirming their separateness. Particularly apposite is Medeiros e Albuquerque's statement included in João do Rio's *O momento literário*—however self-serving it may be, since, of course, he is defending his own decision to accept professionalization:

Generally speaking, the prejudice of littérateurs against journalism is the same that easel painters feel for signboard painters, or sculptors for gravestone chiselers ... Every time practitioners of a trade use the resources of any art for industrial purposes, the followers of the art in question are indignant and systematically disparage the tradesmen who thus become their neighbors. The greater the similarity, the greater the danger that tradesmen will be mistaken for artists, and all the more emphatically artists will express their contempt and try to dig a deep trench between the two realms. (Rio n.d.: 76)

At times this "trench" consisted in little more than mild accusations of levity, inconstancy, and garrulousness directed at the press, as in this 1907 verse *crônica* by Bilac:

> I love you when,
> Gossipy and watchful,
> You go about raising curtains,
> Applying your sharp ear to the walls,
> Your piercing eye to every chink,
> Muffling your firm steps as you go,

> Making an open book of other people's lives,
> Placing on every bit of news
> A buzzing hive of busy-bodied bees ...
> —I love you when Artists and Poets
> Neglect their lawful wife, Dame Art,
> And on the ever generous fresh lips
> You offer smilingly
> Seek the delicious, never-ending,
> Sweet kisses of Unfaithfulness ...
>
> (Pontes 1944: 413–14)

In this rhymed *crônica*, the press is no longer excoriated as it was in the 1897 text in which the devil himself condemned a writer to "write for the papers for the rest of [his] days." Here the criticism is quite mild—the press is gently slapped on the wrist for being "gossipy"—and the relationship between Poets and the press is described as an amorous one—more exactly, as an amorous triangle. The third element here is Art, the Poet's legitimate wife, who is occasionally neglected in favor of the "sweet kisses" of the press. But however mild the criticism implied by this allegorical triangle, still Bilac seems to find it necessary to draw a sharp line between Art and the press. It is as if he wished to make the same point he had established, in "artistic" language, in the poems "O tear" and "A um poeta," included in *Tarde*, to reaffirm the opposition between craftsmanship and technical production, between "creation" and "manufacture," the latter being understood as referring to Bilac's abundant journalistic output.

In fact, the affirmation of this opposition seems to follow inevitably the hegemony of the press in Brazilian intellectual life at the turn of the century and in the first few decades of the twentieth century. This hegemony is evident, for instance, in the obligatory references to the press in Artur Azevedo's yearly revues. In those shows, sometimes the different sections of a newspaper appeared as characters, explaining their own functions: the editorial, the "by-request," the feuilleton novel, and so on. Or representatives of the various newspapers and magazines of Rio de Janeiro would appear onstage to discuss the current situation of the press.

Here is another example. On July 29, 1914, at a time when the late-nineteenth-century rage for literary lectures was already in decline, an evening of "spoken journalism" was held at Rio's Teatro Fênix, promoted by the magazine *Ilustração Brasileira*.[15] For two hours, a newspaper was presented to the audience, all of it illustrated by Calixto Cordeiro, beginning with the "Literary *Crônica*" (João do Rio) and proceeding with the "Political Article" (Costa Rego), the "Congressional Report" (Batista Júnior), the "Humor Department" (Bastos Tigre), the "Theatrical Review" (Oscar Guanabarino), and finally the "Society Column" (Paulo Gardênia).

"There is no power greater / Than the power of the Press," sang a choir of newspapers in *O Carioca*, the 1886 revue by Artur Azevedo and Moreira Sampaio. By 1914 this power seemed to be even greater; for whereas in the yearly revues the press appeared in only a few scenes, in the "spoken journalism" evening the newspaper reigned supreme.

The newspaper created reputations. In Vaz's *Professor Jeremias*, the eponymous hero becomes fleetingly famous for the articles and sonnets he publishes in the *Correio de Pirasseguera* under the anagrammatical pen name of Mejerias: "In the pages of the *Correio* . . . I constantly fanned, in the pyre of our love, the embers of my own renown" (Vaz 1920: 79), Jeremias recalls, sarcastically; for if his later existence did not wholly sink into oblivion, it was because his name once appeared in an errata appended to an "Annual List of Public Servants." His earlier fame, on the strength of publications heavily influenced by Coelho Neto, is seen ironically, all the more so because the novel is written in a direction opposite to that of publicity and deals with a completely and purposely obscure life, one that left no trace.

Jeremias is then the very opposite of Jacques Pedreira, the hero of João do Rio's 1911 novel, who seems to have stepped right out of an illustrated magazine. In fact, everything in *A profissão de Jacques Pedreira* seems to be the polar opposite of *O professor Jeremias*: there is practically no room for dim existences; everything is grist for the papers' mill, and everyone can be the subject of a newspaper photograph. Fittingly, the novel abounds with characters such as the fictional, omnipresent *cronista* Godofredo de Alencar and other journalists, part of the action takes place in editorial rooms, and mention is made of the power of the press over the fates of the various characters—from the millionaire Jorge de Araújo, who showers praise on all reporters because they can both harm him and provide him with business, to the parvenue Alice dos Santos, who studies the precise gestures and the "technology of the haut monde" by leafing through the magazines. When Jorge the chauffeur is killed in an automobile race, Jacques rushes to check the newspapers and see how they covered the accident, although he despises reporters. He finds out that the coverage has been as bad as he feared. "The reporters, the journalists, the anonymous workers of those papers, indirectly forced to serve the caste to which he belonged, and despising it, had their revenge whenever they could" (Rio 1911: 231). Whether or not it was the newsmen's revenge, the fact is that Jacques gets such bad press that he is forced to embark on a diplomatic career. Unlike the "Mejerias" who publishes his literary efforts in the *Correio de Pirassaguera* but is preserved for posterity in an errata, Jacques's fame is achieved not by writing sonnets and articles but simply by making a few personal contacts.

To give another example from João do Rio, in his later novel *A correspondência de uma estação de cura* (1918) one feels that the presence of journalism is seen not only in the plot but also in the author's appropriation of journalistic language in his narrative technique. The short letters that make up the novel are changed into news items covering everyday life in Poços de Caldas, and the whole book becomes a sort of newspaper, a novelized version of a journal. There is the "society column" (letters of Antero Pedreira), the "theatrical review" (letters by José Bento), news reports and "literary *crônicas*" (letters by Teodomiro Pacheco). And the hotel doorman, Troponoff, who conceals the entire correspondence and is described by Teodomiro as "a brilliant journalist," is the fanciful representation of an editor-in-chief, or even of the language standardization encouraged by newspapers.

For, unlike Lima Barreto, João do Rio does not exactly elaborate on journalistic resources in his prose; rather, he self-consciously reproduces features of some journalistic genres and incorporates into his work the clear and straightforward language of reportage. And, unlike Bilac and Coelho Neto, he intersperses dialogues with the medium with ornamental excess.

João do Rio has his prejudices as well, but they are mostly directed at journalists who lack "literary background," as he makes clear in "O charuto das Filipinas":

Your average citizen fails in every profession, goes broke, is dropped by his own gambling club. What to do? He becomes a journalist. That charming young man, whose purse is as depleted of bills as his mind is filled with the desire to frequent the higher social circles, suddenly finds himself at the brink of the abyss. What does he do? Unhesitatingly, he becomes a journalist. (Rio 1909: 262)

And he goes on to name a number of other "disreputable" types who wind up as journalists, from "cunning industrialists" to political hopefuls, from racketeers to engineers, admirals, and ne'er-do-wells. "Members of every social class, from barbers to gentlemen members of the Club dos Diários," he writes, "are perpetually hoping, whenever they speak to a stranger, that this stranger might turn out to be a journalist" (p. 262).

In José Agudo's *Gente rica* there is an even more biting caricature of social-climbing would-be journalists. Juvenal de Faria, the only penniless character in a novel abounding with rich people, not only refuses to take up journalism as a profession but also sees it—not unlike the protagonist of Lima Barreto's *Recordações do escrivão Isaías Caminha*, who is only a little less bitter about it—as a mixture of influence-seeking, boondoggling, and boot-licking.

> "Well," his friends would say, changing the subject, "if you really don't care to be anything, as you say, you could at least become a journalist—be an opinion-maker!"
>
> "I'm too old to go about on all fours. My joints are too stiff. I've been told it's arthritis."
>
> "What do you mean, go about on all fours?"
>
> "You can't go into the press in any other way. The cult of the sacred organs of Public Opinion is quite incompatible with an upright posture, my dear fellows." (Agudo 1912: 60)

Though his character Juvenal is cynical about the press, José Agudo is influenced by its forms in ways he is perhaps unaware of. Parts of the novel are literally short *crônicas* juxtaposed (for instance, Chapter 7, "Variazone," a digression about the "neurosis of speed"); the very division of the book into short chapters, some of them little more than brief jokes; the characters, most of whom are representative of various kinds of successful crookedness and are like caricatures in prose—everything smacks of journalism. Thus Agudo's situation contrasts with that of Bilac, who, though he tried to develop stylistic forms that could resist the new forms of communication that in practice failed to resist them successfully, nevertheless was in favor of professionalization in journalism. Agudo's novel, however, testifies to the ever-growing influence of the press on literary language even as it cast a critical eye on journalism as a profession. While Juvenal refuses to yield to his friends' pressures, José Agudo writes under the increasingly strong impact of the standardization of language imposed by the major newspapers.

Reelaboration in Lima Barreto, "unconscious" mimesis in José Agudo, rejection through overornamentation in Coelho Neto and Alberto de Oliveira or through affirmation of the narrator's function in *Vida ociosa*, conscious mimesis in João do Rio—all of these literary procedures show the telltale marks of modern technique on Brazilian literary production in the 1920's and 1930's. These include the influence of newspaper layout, cuts, sharper writing with less ornamentation (adjectives, scientific jargon, and picturesque regional terms).

It should be remembered that Oswald de Andrade used journalistic resources in his literary work and refused to draw a sharp line between the two kinds of writing. Relevant examples are his "letters in macaronic Portuguese," published under the pen name "Annibale Scipione," and the first fragments of *Memórias sentimentais de João Miramar*, published in 1917, both in the magazine *O Pirralho*. The staccato rhythm of his prose seems to be at least partly based on the short sentences of newspaper copy, with its cuts and brief paragraphs. Oswald's fragmentation, his "telegraphic style," seemed closely associated with the conciseness and simultaneity of the newspaper.

In her study of Oswald's newspaper writing, Chalmers (1976) mentions that the influence of journalism can be found even in his early novel *Os condenados* (1922), which is not divided into chapters in the conventional way:

The search for simultaneity in the book violates the logical and causal order of exposition; in the same way, news items are often written in such a way that no rigid structure is followed, since the order in which the information is presented is irrelevant for the purpose at hand. This sort of open text is a result of the acceleration of speed in the transmission of information via telegraph. (Chalmers 1976: 80)[16]

This "telegraphic style" is then directly modeled on journalistic writing. Much the same could be said of Alcântara Machado's *Pathé Baby* or Juó Bananére's witty wordplay in his *La divina increnca* (1915).[17]

Oswald's writings for the press of the 1910's also suggest a less evolutionistic approach to the relations between literature and technology. Naturally, as the new technological landscape that comes to dominate cities since the late nineteenth century becomes more familiar, its treatment in literature is correspondingly affected. Once the initial astonishment and fascination are gone, and the unsettling impact on traditional literary forms is gradually assimilated, it becomes possible for literature to develop a more critical and articulate relation with technical processes of reproduction and the images generated by them. However, it should be kept in mind that it was in the early twentieth century, when this technological landscape was still being formed, that some of the possible literary responses (later discarded, reappropriated, or reevaluated) were devised.

There is a tendency to think of the relation between literature and journalism from the late nineteenth century to the early twentieth century in terms of a trivialization of art, a decay of taste, or the like. But it is possible to approach the literature produced in this period from a somewhat different angle. Given the fact that a new technological world was in the making, one that was to have a direct impact on forms of perception as well as on how texts were printed and distributed, it becomes difficult to see the production of the period merely in terms of earlier or later "literary" trends.

In the case of Brazilian literature of the period, technology is a variable that cannot be left out in any evaluation of it. For the interlocutors of this literature are not simply the naturalism of yesterday and the modernism of tomorrow. The tension that is the source of the reportagelike letters of *A correspondência de uma estação de cura*, of the chapter titles proposed by Lobato for Godofredo Rangel's *Vida ociosa*, or even of the countless ornamental words in Coelho Neto's texts, is not intertextual only. There is also a direct or indirect interplay with the new forms of printing, reproduction, and distribution, as well as with the conditions under which intellectual work took place in the period, which helped shape the literary technique of the authors of the period, from the way their characters are constructed to the notion of time that came to characterize novels; from the reconstruction of the profile of the narrator to the replacement of the traditional narrator by a succession of montage operations; from the preference for a poetry of interiors to a literature of signboards. I now examine these possibilities.

CHAPTER 4

Literary Technique

As we have seen, it is possible to trace, in the literature of the period, the history of the attempt to implement modern technology in Brazil since the late nineteenth century. One can also see, in the literary works in question, the marks—some subtle, others quite clear—of these new forms of reproduction and diffusion of images and sounds. But there is no one-to-one correspondence between the two sets of traces. One could not say that it is precisely where these changes of perspective and sensibility are directly treated that the dialogue between literature and technology leads to significant changes in literary technique. Nor would it be true to say that new literary techniques are necessarily present whenever literary text attempts either to mimic or to disguise (by means of overornamentation) the processes of reproduction, the genres, the language, or the layout of the new industrialized press and the newborn advertising industry. For, in addition to pointing out the marks of the new technical resources and new forms of perception—sometimes disguised or presented as inverted mirror images—it is also necessary to include in the picture something that stirs in the background and seems somehow to resist explicit descriptions, a different set of traces, more subtle, displaced, even indifferent to whether their presence is detected.

In addition to the attempt to bring literary language closer to that of journalism, to capture the speed of mechanical motion or the "faithful reproduction of life" in the images of photography and film, to convey the impression of accelerated time that was increasingly present since the 1880's, there were other, less mimetic, relations between literary form and modern technology. In addition to the sort of writing that mimicked the poster, there was a second literature that stylized its own contacts with industry and the market, and advertised itself as pure ornament. And, on a third plane, apparently unconnected to the other two, there was another kind of literary diction, neither ornament nor poster, one that made few references to modernization, urban reform, or diffusion of industrial artifacts in Brazil. This literature relied neither on imitation nor on ornamentation but on a quite different procedure: displacement.

Thus we have three paradigmatic paths. The new technologies of the period—phonographs, daguerreotypy, biographs, and photochemical printing methods—became increasingly important after the implementation of electric power networks that began in the 1910's and came to have a decisive influence on cultural production and reproduction in Brazil; their impact on literary technique may be seen in terms of three basic procedures: *imitation, stylization,* and *displacement.*

Imitation includes the use of the surface-only genres, diction, and characters typical of newspapers and illustrated magazines and of the fiction, plays, and *crônicas* of João do Rio; the resort to topicality and news in Bilac's feuilletons and his *crônicas* in verse; and the unconscious mimesis to be found in the journalistic language sometimes employed by José Agudo in his *Gente rica,* for instance.

Stylization includes the reelaboration of resources characteristic of journalism—redundancy in Lima Barreto, and reportage in Euclides da Cunha's *Os sertões* (Rebellion in the backlands, 1902); the conversion of the "experience of shock" caused by early modernization into an endless series of "ohs!," interjections, exclamations, and vocatives, a sort of ornamental astonishment, common in Bilac's *crônicas*; and the emphasis on literary "craftsmanship" dramatizing its opposition to industrial "standardization," manifestations of which are the oratory of the period, Parnassian poetry, symbolist prose, and much of Coelho Neto's work. This emphasis is a curious manifestation, since industrialization in Brazil did not replace a locally well-established tradition of craftsmanship, which had never really developed on account of slavery (see Carvalho 1987: 138). But in the sphere of literature it is possible to detect in this period a transition from a type of production "in the king's shadow" to the beginnings of professionalization via the press and the advertising industry. At the same time, there was a transition from a sort of "artisanal" writing— that is, actually written by hand and published in very small editions—to the kind of "serial writing" demanded by the press.

As for displacement, numerous examples can be found in the work of Afonso Arinos. It operates fundamentally in three directions, by privileging as characters—or as elements in the narrative—tokens (an eighteenth-century sedan chair, an isolated muriti palm in the grasslands, an old lady reminiscing), types (the backlands thug, the emperor), or feelings (nostalgia, tearfulness) that are somehow out of context. Ever the antiquarian, Arinos speaks of remnants of a bygone grandeur. His fiction emphasizes genres characterized by displacement, whether in time—historical novels such as *Os jagunços* (1898) and *O contratador de diamantes*—or in space—the backwoods tales of *Pelo sertão* (1898) and the folklore of *Lendas e tradições brasileiras* (1917).

Even more common than the historical novel, however, was the use of reminiscences—displacement through memory; examples are such novels as Raul Pompéia's *O Ateneu*, Léo Vaz's *O professor Jeremias*, autobiographical writings such as Joaquim Nabuco's *Minha formação* (1900) and Coelho Neto's *A conquista* (1899); and such fictionalized versions of the memoirs as Machado de Assis's *Memórias póstumas de Brás Cubas* (Epitaph for a small winner, 1881) and Oswald de Andrade's *Memórias sentimentais de João Miramar*, parts of which were already being published as early as 1917.

The memoirs and essayistic novels of the period—examples of the latter genre being Gonzaga Duque's *Mocidade morta* (1899) and Hilário Tácito's *Madame Pommery* (1920)—at a time when the decisive influence of journalistic diction seemed to suggest the gradual weakening of the figure of the narrator, point in the opposite direction, to the affirmation of subjectivity, as manifested in reminiscences or digressions. The same could be said of the painstaking reconstruction of the narrator in a book like Rangel's *Vida ociosa* or in the many poetical "interiors" of the penumbrista poets or of Augusto dos Anjos's *Eu*.

Another expression of displacement in time took place not in the choice of genre but in the very structure of the narrative. It was as if the acceleration of historical time, the sensation of a "present in constant motion," corresponded in fiction to a different kind of writing, one that moved to a different rhythm. Thus the days flow slowly in *Vida ociosa*, and the time scale of legend governs Simões Lopes Neto's lovely stories; thus the phrase "let us bide our time" is repeated as a kind of leitmotif in Valdomiro Silveira's *Os caboclos* (1920), in clear contrast with the "haste to get it over with" that characterized not only the day-to-day existence of potential readers but also their "absentminded reception," the impact of the *crônica* on literary production (including the criticism) of the period.

Displacement—not in the sense of establishing a contrast between fiction and everyday existence, but in the sense of reaffirming experience—is also present in the spatialization of time effected by the yearly revues of Aluísio Azevedo, Artur Azevedo, Moreira Sampaio, Oscar Pederneiras, Valentim Magalhães, and Arlindo Leal. It is also apparent in the (perhaps unconscious) representation of the growing influence of technical reproduction and such mass media as the newspaper in mediating characters like Godofredo de Alencar and the barão de Belfort, who are constant presences in João do Rio's work, constructing and deconstructing plots, commenting on widely varying topics, acting as secondary narrators in all the texts they appear in. Another example of displacement can be found in the *raisonneurs* that emerge in the proletarian drama of the early twentieth century (for instance, a French play, staged in Italian, called *Responsabilità*, or José Oiticica's *Pedra que rola*). The *raisonneurs*, adapted from bourgeois drama, were characters who stood outside the action to explain it and tell spectators how they were supposed to understand what they were seeing.[1] Though ideologically there was a sharp contrast between the *raisonneurs* of proletarian drama and João do Rio's Godofredo and Belfort, their function was precisely the same: to act as mediators both between different characters and situations and between the text and its potential receptors, whether the setting was the world of labor or the haut monde of Rio.

A different kind of mediation was provided in the urban setting by the growing popularity of metal structures and iron architectural components in the major Brazilian cities since the late nineteenth century (see Silva 1986). The display of construction materials, or even of the iron structure itself (as in the building of the Livraria Universal in Belém) is analogous to the mediation of *raisonneurs* in different literary and theatrical genres of the period. And it is reminiscent of yet another kind of mediation, not directly named, but displaced and singularized in iron architecture and stage *raisonneurs*, a kind of mediation that was growing increasingly familiar: that of the modern media for the reproduction, printing, and massive diffusion of technical images, texts, voices, and advertisements. These media brought to literary technique and sensibility new ways of conceiving time, character, narration, and subjectivity. And the very act of writing also became subject to mechanical mediation: typewriters were popularized and widely advertised in magazines and leaflets, particularly beginning in the 1910's.

Dance of the Hours

" 'To bide one's time' is a phrase whose meaning has been completely lost. One no longer has time for anything," João do Rio observes (Rio 1909: 386). "Bide your time, man! This notion that nobody don't love you just on account of somethin' bad that's happened to somebody or a fallin' out that's happened to somebody else is nothin' more than poppycock!" a character observes in the story "Cena de amor," included in *Os caboclos* (Silveira 1962: 1). The mere juxtaposition of these two passages brings out the tension in the manner of representing time, under the pressure of a flowing present, a sharp awareness of time as extremely fast movement. While the *cronista* attempts to incorporate into his own writing the haste that is characteristic of urban life, the regionalist writer tries to reconstruct the unhurried pace of the backwoods.

These different representations directly influence the actual structure of the plot. In Valdomiro Silveira's story "Por mexericos," for instance, "biding one's time" has the effect of avoiding disasters, as the narrative makes clear:

For a long time he stood there, without a word, with a whole load of rage and blame: and it was just as well that he waited for so long, seething in silence, for so it was that he placed a hand on his own shoulder, and measured out the words he was to say, and weighed the consequences, and balanced one against the other. (Silveira 1962: 6)

A much more significant consequence, from the standpoint not of the plot but of the narration, is the expansion of the present time that characterizes Godofredo Rangel's *Vida ociosa*. Practically half of the novel describes a single day, Dr. Félix's visit to the Córrego Fundo farm, where Américo, Próspero, and Marciana live. On this farm, life is marked by "Marciana's dragging of slippers" and "a most delicious slowness." Félix explains: "Time stood still, the world froze on the last crossing of hands, the last syllable of a voice, as in the castle of the sleeping princess, life was suspended on the last emotion, the beating of the heart in a diastole, everything drifted into a state of dreamy unreality" (Rangel n.d.: 71). The characters' movements are slow and deliberate; their conversation is a succession of anecdotes and reminiscences told at the most leisurely pace imaginable. Even the narrator, a jurist, "a new species of vampire" and therefore a man on a different temporal wavelength, is pervaded by this slowness, by the near motionlessness of time, best exemplified by the fishing scenes and the fireside conversations. His very way of narrating is influenced, so that his story is full of digressions, carefully described details, long pauses—a self-consciously "written" narration, a writing whose pictorial equivalent in the novel is given by Américo's drawings.

For when the narrator speaks of the numerous sketches of fish made by his friend he seems to be referring, though unconsciously, to his own attitude. This much is made clear by the moment chosen by Américo to make his drawings and by Dr. Félix to present his narrative. While Américo depicts the fish at the very moment when, having been hooked out of the river, they are being taken to the kitchen, Félix describes life on the farm as one who is consciously talking about things on the brink of extinction—not "dead objects," in the manner of Afonso Arinos, but unlikely survivors of a different time, on their way to oblivion. Like Américo in *Vida ociosa*, Rangel describes these relics with the painstaking care of a craftsman, attempting somehow to capture these dying forms. "Life-size dourados, twenty-inch piabas, gigantic catfish with their barbels still stirring and their fins fanning out" cover the walls; stories of fishing and hunting expeditions, siestas, and homemade delicacies follow one another in a narrative that attempts to capture them in its own terms. In a literary environment, these elements are converted into forces of resistance against not only extinction but also an absentminded, hasty sort of reading, and a prose that is closer to reportage than to invention.

Thus the description of Américo's drawings and primitive craftsmanship may be seen as Rangel's representation of his own calligraphic writing. Recounts Dr. Félix: "Américo had an uncanny talent for making—out of bamboo, pieces of spools, and sheets of mica—whimsically shaped pens, dyed with annatto and shoemaker's powder, earth yellow with black stripes" (Rangel n.d.: 35). The text not only describes the work of craftsmanship undertaken by the character, analogous to that of the calligrapher-narrator, but also displays similar features itself. To quote from Antonio Candido's 1953 essay, where he groups Rangel, Léo Vaz, Ciro dos Anjos, Amadeu de Queirós, and Eduardo Frieiro together as the "calligraphers":

Their books seem to display, on every line, beneath the monotony of typography, a manuscript lovingly traced by hand, in accordance with the ancient art that was gradually lost with the advent first of the press, then of the typewriter, but whose spirit survives in their style, animating, like the lost but living leaf of a palimpsest, the impersonal shape of the printed letter. (Candido 1984: 3)

Calligraphic writing is thus contrasted with the standardization of journalistic language that characterized the period. By reinforcing the function of the narrator and widening the scope of the present, carefully shaping his sentences in loving detail, Godofredo Rangel reacts to the modernization of urban life, the diffusion of new industrial artifacts, and the growing professionalization of men of letters. This reaction also took place in the sphere of architecture, as though it were necessary to display, in a fast-changing cityscape filled with signboards and advertisements, a different kind of inscription. Calligraphy was a reaction to the standardized illustration of billboards. Hence the numerous monograms and elaborate dates found in façades and friezes of stores and residences in Rio de Janeiro, particularly since the last years of the nineteenth century. According to some, these were manifestations of the proprietor's pride in "belonging to a modern age."[2] But perhaps they should be seen instead as a way of singularizing buildings, of leaving one's personal mark at a time when the tendency was to erase such marks.

Though in *Vida ociosa* the present time is expanded and the pace of time is slowed down, the more common solution seems to have been the attempt, sometimes desperate, to capture the fleeting instant. This explains the increasing vitality of such genres as the *crônica*, the rhymed columns, and the yearly revues. Other examples of this emphasis on the instant as a form of perception and representation of time are some of the "snapshots in verse" by Bilac, Artur Azevedo, and Emílio de Meneses published in the papers. Here is a quatrain by Meneses that came out in *A Imprensa* in 1911 under the pen name "Zangão," next to the news that in Recife rioters had destroyed the wiring of the lampposts:

> The Dantistas surely have
> A number of admirable virtues,
> But Positivists they are not:
> Enlightenment's not their forte.
> (Meneses 1980: 177)

In this example, poetry does no more than repeat, in a humorous vein, the content of the news item. Usually only very recent events were glossed in verse; hardly ever was mention made of anything that had taken place even a few months earlier. Thus it was immediately after two employees of the Light and Power Company had embezzled a large sum that *A Imprensa* published the following sonnet, also by Meneses, on March 3, 1912:

> When I read of matters such as these
> I'm—well, not *happy*, but grateful, rather;
> for the *Light Company*, that soaring eagle,
> always reduces our Government to a sparrow!
>
> The people—young or old, wealthy or poor—
> are ever willing to let *Light* have its way,
> and Light, rapacious—even *Lloyd* it covets!—
> catches with its beak every bird it sees.
>
> The *Light and Power Company*
> in broad daylight wields its power
> and little cares for what we think of it.
>
> Not always, though. *This* time, it seems,
> its light is dimmed, its power fails,
> and two sparrows bring the mighty eagle down!
>
> (Pp. 183–84)

Some of the poems included by B. Lopes in his *Brasões* (1895) follow the model of the society column rather than that of the news item. Here is an example, the sonnet "Turfe":

> It's Sunday. Green below, and blue above,
> And the crystal of morn quiv'ring in between;
> The sun is like some golden rattle, full
> Of the sonorous delight of a rhyme.
>
> A fine day for a bout of fencing,
> For brandishing foils in bold swift strokes
> That tone one's muscles, while the blood
> Draws patches of purpura on one's breast;
>
> Or for a two-mile *tour de champ*
> In a fleet phaeton, drawn by a lusty mare,
> Sleek and shiny, like some glossy chromo;
>
> And as the flower of society looks on
> One storms around the hippodrome
> Like an enormous, blazing grenade!

Such texts, based on a fragmentary perception of time and ever attempting to capture the passing moment, use language as no more than a flexible frame that can accommodate different approaches to a continuous present, similar to the present that is the stuff of journalistic writing. For the simple fact that they are working in newspapers—and thus are in contact with the view of a single day as a privileged condensation of history—seems to suggest to these poets a literary form that is evocative of transience, grounded in the newspaper. This form is undemanding, pleasant, and adequate to represent everyday topics gracefully; and it respects the omnipotence of the present moment, its models being the *crônica* and the snapshot.

Bilac's Parnassian poetry approaches time from the opposite angle, but with a literary language that is just as lax, although overornamented. In contrast with his "Gazeta rimada" and with the ephemeral present of the newspaper, Bilac attempts to reinvigorate eternity as a time coordinate not only for a would-be classical literary production but also for the urban experience. Thus when he expresses his fascination for New York City he cannot suppress a note of condemnation in the sonnet's closing tercets, where the city is described from the angle of eternity:

> For all thy Babels, 'tis in vain thou scrap'st
> The skies, and weigh'st upon the seas
> As thou evok'st the memory of hundred-gated Thebes:
>
> 'Tis Time thou wantest—the vague, religious whiff
> That wafts in the air of Roma and Lutetia,
> That ancient, ever-young perfume of bygone ages ...
>
> (Bilac 1919: 122–23)

In Bilac's "serious" poetry, then, there is no attempt to make the time of the text reflect the haste of urban time, or to expand the present moment; rather, the urge is to abandon historical time in favor of an "eternal" vantage point from which to see the desire for modernization that characterized the period. This displacement of viewpoint is particularly evident in the following sonnet on the cyclical return of a comet:

> A comet passed ... In light, on cliffs,
> In grass and insects, in all a soul shone forth;
> The Earth enslaved herself to the Sun;
> Blood and sap did boil. And the comet fled ...
>
> The land was racked by earthquakes, lava,
> Floods, cyclones, wars, famine and plague;
> But love was born again, and pride as well,
> Religions came and went ... And the comet passed,
>
> And fled, and shook its golden tail ...
> A race died out; and hardy loneliness
> Bred a new race afresh. And the comet returned ...

The fearsome clangor of the ages rushed on,
And all, from stone to man, proclaimed
Its own eternity! And the comet smiled ...
(Bilac 1919: 170–71)

Transitory things are listed: wars, plagues, races, loves, religions; all of these pass. However, one seemingly eternal element persists: the comet. This seems to suggest that Bilac, facing the corrosive action of time, arms himself with multiple representations of eternity, which are particularly tranquilizing for those readers who have not yet become used to the amazements of modernization, the reshaped urban landscape, the ever-growing presence of industrially produced technical artifacts in their everyday lives.

The instant, eternity, the slowing down of the present: here are three forms of representing and understanding time—mimicking everyday experience, proposing a different pace for it, or replacing it altogether—typical of Brazilian cultural production from the 1890's to the 1920's. These representations are engaged in a dialogue with the technical reproduction of movement and the modern sense of time as constant speedy motion; sometimes they submit to their interlocutors, and at other times they anxiously attempt to disguise or forget them. Sometimes the latter alternative leads to excellent literary results, as in the case of Simões Lopes Neto's regionalistic prose.

Lopes Neto is largely concerned with a different time axis: his stories are marked by the imaginary time of legend, a time with no calendars. The opening passage of "A MBoitatá" is emblematic:

It was like this: a long, long time ago there was a night so long it didn't seem as if there was ever going to be daylight again.

A pitch-black dark night, with no stars in the sky, no wind, no dew, no noises, no smells of ripe pastures or wild flowers. (Lopes Neto 1957: 281)[3]

Even when there is a more definite time scale, as in the story "Chasque do Imperador" from the collection *Contos gauchescos* (1912), the point of departure for which is "the Paraguayan siege of Uruguaiana in 1865," something about the text resists historical time. Here what really sets the time as well as the pace of the narrative is the "telling of one's own experience," the narrator's profile. The narrator in question is Blau Nunes, the scout.

"If you was someone who was alive back then, I wouldn't tell you about it, 'cause it would all be old news to you, but next to me you're as good as a child, seeing as I could be your grandpa ... So listen ... " (Lopes Neto 1957: 163). These are the opening words of "Correr eguada," another of Lopes Neto's Gaucho tales. Blau explains that what is actually taking place in them is a conversation with a reader-listener of a different time, in which experiences are described and a distant age is built on the meanderings of memory and speech. The narrative is sometimes interrupted—"You'll excuse the delay, but when you meet someone you know from a long time ago, and when it's someone as big as that ... " (p. 188), Blau says in "Melancia—coco verde" after leaving his interlocutor for a while—sometimes purposely repetitious—"There's nothing like drinking mate and rounding up some mares!," he exclaims, then shortly after repeats: "There's nothing like drinking mate and rounding up some mares, like in the old days!"—and sometimes indulges in short digressions. The narrative wavers back and forth consciously, on its own time, a time that is constructed in a literary way, quite different from that of everyday perception.

In Lopes Neto, as in Godofredo Rangel's calligraphic writing, what is important is that this contrast between the time of the narrative and the everyday experience of a "floating present" is accompanied by changes in the actual form of the narration. This contrast attempts to counter the tendency to suppress the presence of the narrator in the name of "objective" reportage—which was already evident in a novel such as João do Rio's *A correspondência de uma estação de cura*, for instance.

This is not to say that João do Rio's novel is inferior to *Vida ociosa*. Given his choice of a literary technique that mimics journalistic language, João do Rio uses his resources quite successfully; examples of his skill are his suppression of the name of the "editor" up to the very end and his mixture of journalistic genres in the letters that make up the novel. Rangel, in turn, contrasts literary writing with the new technical developments and emphasizes the slowness of time implied by modernity, and in so doing tightens the traditional way of reading fictional texts, expanding not only the present time of the narrative but also the moment of reading. His procedure is similar to that of Lopes Neto, who, however, rather than expand the present, brings forth another, legendary, time. Thus these authors create, among their potential public, zones of attrition, usually neglected possibilities of slower paces, of "taking one's time."

When one considers the critic Tristão de Ataíde's comment to the effect that there was at the time a clear preference for short texts, lectures, and *crônicas* at the expense of the full-length book and more demanding texts, one becomes aware of the importance of the challenge to literary reception effected by Rangel and Lopes Neto. Wrote Ataíde in "O pré-modernismo de 1919 a 1920": "The intense and confusing life of ideas, the ever-changing situations, the fads, the scientific and practical discoveries and applications, the vertiginous rapids of the world's course today will not accept any delay in the transmission of ideas" (Fiorentino 1982: 42). This, together with "the difficulties of typographical printing, has given magazines, lectures, courses, and newspapers a new literary edge over books," which, in the case of Brazil, had the following consequences:

Among us, there is a growing preference for writing that comes in short installments, that makes no great demands on patience, investigation, observation, and polish, qualities that are not in harmony with our national life. This, it seems, is the reason why the great bulk of our literary production consists of *crônicas*, lectures, articles, and speeches, more even than poetry. (P. 42)

This preference for absentminded reception and short, undemanding texts was also observed by José Agudo, somewhat sarcastically, in *Gente rica*: "Learning without studying, getting rich without working, becoming famous without merit, flaunting with no substance: these are the modern ideals" (Agudo 1912: 149–50). João do Rio makes much the same point, though not as bitterly, in "A pressa de acabar," commenting on the theater audience:

Regard the theatergoer. By the middle of the last act he is already nervous, eager to leave. Why? To have a quick cup of chocolate. Why quick? To take the streetcar, where we can see him fidgeting at the first bottleneck. Why? Because he is in a hurry to go to bed, to get up early, and hurriedly proceed with the fast moves of his fleeting existence! (Rio 1909: 385)

Both in the hectic quickening of this breakneck pace—as exemplified by Oswald de Andrade's "telegraphic style"—and in its careful slowing down by Rangel and Lopes Neto, the reader is made aware of his or her hasty reception and also, at the same time, is confronted with the possibility of deautomatizing this haste and other processes associated with it. Among the latter are the erasure of the traces of the narrator and the creation of "surface-only characters," to which are counterposed shadowy interiors and journeys into memory, whether fictional or biographical. We shall now examine this tension.

Surface-Only Characters

Words describing landscapes: this was the naturalistic game. "Landscape," whether urban or clinical, was understood as reality in the raw, to be imitated just as it was—with all the necessary exercises of perspective or visual sleight-of-hand, of course. But photographs, signboards, photochemical printing methods, cylinders and engraved plates, advertising leaflets, and illustrated magazines added up to an altogether different game. For by the end of the century a new landscape was superimposing itself on the earlier one and, as it did so, introducing alternative definitions of reality, image, and representation. A landscape that aspired to modernity began to outline a two-dimensional, poster-like world of images. Like a poster, this world was structured on the basis of an interplay of lines and contours and planes, a game of surfaces. The possibilities for reproduction and multiplication of these surfaces were unpredictable and endless.

Words describing images: this was the new game of Brazilian literature ushered in by the technical innovations of the turn of the century that redefined the notion of reality, now combined with this new, second-nature landscape, which could either transform it or ratify it. This landscape of technically produced images became increasingly familiar in the everyday experience of Brazilians after the 1890's; the same desire for modernization that inspired urban and public health reforms led to the technicalization of Brazilian society, to the creation of this new landscape of posters, photographs, movies, and caricatures, a horizon of images. As Sontag observes:

A society becomes modern when one of its chief activities is producing and consuming images, when images that have extraordinary powers to determine our demands upon reality and are themselves coveted substitutes for firsthand experience become indispensable to the health of the economy, the stability of the polity, and the pursuit of private happiness. (Sontag 1977: 153)

Such was the attempt at modernization that took place in Brazil at this time. It implied the creation of a technically produced landscape of two-dimensional figures, façades, and apparatuses.

But most of the industrial artifacts of the period operated in rather precarious circumstances. A good example of this is given in Frederico Figner's memoirs. Describing his early attempts to combine the images of the kinetoscope with the sounds of the phonograph around 1894 or 1895, he emphasizes the material difficulties he faced:

The whole thing was quite troublesome, for one had to keep recharging twenty-five storage batteries constantly, and since there was no power network I had to send them over to the only electricity store in town, owned by a Mr. Ferreira, a very courteous Portuguese gentleman who did all he could to help me, and later at Joaquim's workshop, on rua Santa Luzia. (Ferreira 1986: 15)

No power network, precarious facilities; small wonder that fires were frequent in the early years of movies in Brazil. There was a minor fire at the theater where Figner was showing a "sylphorama," better known at the time as "Inana." The following item appeared in the July 8, 1898, issue of the *Gazeta de Notícias*: "In the wee hours of this morning, soon after midnight, there was a fire at rua do Ouvidor, 132, where the Inana is being exhibited. The fire started on a table where a phonograph had been placed and was promptly extinguished by firemen" (Araújo 1976: 62). A more serious fire of the period occurred at the Salão Paris, owned by the brothers Gaetano and Pascoal Segreto, at rua do Ouvidor, 141, on August 8, 1898. According to the following day's *Gazeta de Notícias*, the initial blast occurred when "employees were cleaning the engine and the machines that power the apparatus" (p. 109). Fires, explosions, "ineffective distribution of power," faulty electrical installations (a problem that began to be solved in Rio only in 1908, when the Ribeirão das Lajes power station opened): for all these troubles, however, the interest in modern apparatuses for the production and reproduction of images grew stronger. This interest would result in a perception of the world as image and of the image as one more "concrete thing" in a landscape that was to be modernized as quickly as possible.

The growing importance of technically produced images is suggested by the fact that, after the Canudos rebellion was crushed in 1897, the body of the rebel leader Antônio Conselheiro was carefully disinterred so that it could be photographed. For, as Euclides da Cunha observed in his *Rebellion in the Backlands*, it was important to persuade the urban populations that the "Counselor" had been killed and the peasant resistance had been overcome.[4] For this, photography was required. Another instructive instance—a rather curious one—of this moment when technology began to be seen as the paramount way of representing landscapes "with things" is a verse advertisement of the Leterre photographic studio, published in the *Gazeta de Notícias* on July 9, 1900: "Poor Miss L. R. / Was a sad and lonesome spinster. / But LETERRE photographed her / And he gave her such a sweet look / That—and this was done on Wednesday— / By

Thursday she was married" (Araújo 1976: 42). Thus photography did more than just provide proof, as was the case of the image of Antônio Conselheiro or of the many exhibitions of photographs of the Canudos War held in major Brazilian cities soon after the quashing of the rebellion, exhibitions that drew a sizable public. Laterre's ad seems to imply that photographic technique can *create* a different reality: a seductive portrait of a woman can lend her some of its attractiveness and thus change her life decisively.

In this world of images, this history in snapshots that came to characterize the period, the caricatures of well-known figures published by the major newspapers became increasingly important. The starting point is 1896, when the *Gazeta de Notícias* began to run a series of "snapshot caricatures" by Julião Machado, side by side with personal profiles written by Lúcio de Mendonça. Other newspapers soon took up the practice. Lima (1969) notes that in 1898 the *Jornal do Brasil* began to publish caricatures, at first weekly, then daily, and soon on its front page; *O País* and the *Correio da Manhã* followed suit.

In this way, the urban population came to acquire a perception based on surfaces, on two-dimensional areas structured around lines and planes. These surfaces could be photographs, posters, or caricatures; and they seem to have had a decisive impact on the process of character construction in the literature of the period. Outlines are sharply delineated; only the most significant features of situations and characters are represented; the space of caricature presents in condensed fashion only those aspects that make the represented person or situation comical: quick, easily decodable synthesis is the modus operandi of caricaturists.[5] And the *cronista*-like novelists of the period seem to adopt a similar method. Types and situations are sketched out hurriedly, and some characters are presented as veritable caricatures.

In the case of Théo Filho and Benjamin Costallat, authors who were extremely popular in the first few decades of the twentieth century, such caricatured characters are indeed the rule. The characters are mere illustrations in *crônica*-like novels, written to be read with little attention. Even in João do Rio's more elaborate prose they predominate. But there is something painfully explicit about their presence, at times to the extent of causing some discomfort in the reader. Here is a stage direction in his play *Eva* in which João do Rio describes the farmer Souza Prates: "He is a latest-model farmer from one of the most illustrious Sao Paulo families. A member of the São Paulo Automobile Club and of the Paris Aero, filthy rich, slightly snobbish, he leads a life of uninterrupted leisure" (Rio n.d.: 7). The brief character sketch clearly suggests some degree of fascination with the character's wealth and snobbishness, but there is one disturbing detail: the analogy between Souza Prates and a manufactured product. The term "latest-model farmer" evokes an ad for an automobile or some other apparatus, which is advertised for a time until the phrase "latest model" no longer applies to it.

Another unsympathetic profile is that of Sanches in *A correspondência de uma estação de cura*. "They are absolutely figures in a fashion magazine, illustrations in *Vie Heureuse*. One wants to touch them to see whether they are indeed flesh and blood. But Sanchez is making an effort: he is reading (in a richly bound edition) the fifth volume of Victor Hugo's *Les Misérables*" (Rio 1918: 10). The description is thoroughly unkind, and the unkindest cut of all is in the parenthesis: Sanches's sole attempt to escape being an illustration in *Vie Heureuse* is mocked when we are told that what really matters is not the work itself but the book's binding. Characters who are absolutely figures in a fashion magazine read books that are absolutely richly bound editions.

Another such character is Alice dos Santos in *A profissão de Jacques Pereira*. The wife of a provincial politician and Jacques's lover, she aspires for a modernization of the sort that Rio is undergoing and forges a worldview and an external image for herself solely on the basis of magazines and newspapers. In just a few words João do Rio sketches a merciless caricature of Alice dos Santos:

The care with which she compared herself with the photographs of the *grandes dames* in the illustrated sheets, always concluding that she was the better looking! The tenacity with which she studied in the worldly magazines the technology, the confusing language of the haute monde—in fact, such a limited world! (Rio 1911: 68)

But such characters as Sanches, Souza Prates, and Alice dos Santos are meant as figures in a fashion magazine. And though João do Rio seems to delight in caricature, his pen is somewhat less harsh when he depicts a character who spins off *crônicas* apropos of everything. Godofredo de Alencar is less of a caricature; but he remains two-dimensional in a different sense: his is the two-dimensionality of the printed page. Whether caricatures or *crônicas*, these characters are defined in terms of a technical landscape; and they act as antagonists in relation to other trends in the Brazilian prose and poetry of the period.

It is then under the sign of memory (whether romanced or biographical) and in opposition to "sandwich men," "men without ideals," and men who are nothing more than their own fame that *O Ateneu*, *Recordações do escrivão Isaías Caminha*, and *O professor Jeremias* were written, respectively. These books are journeys into memory conceived as a way of rethinking the role of the narrator, which at the time was being reduced to no more than a photo reproduction. Thus the figure of the grandfather in *O professor Jeremias*, for instance, dwindles to a portrait in a living room—and a portrait whose importance is diminished by its placement next to that of a public personage: President Floriano Peixoto. Rather timorously, then, an attempt is made to restore subjectivity and forms of narrating and configuring the lyrical self that seem to be threatened with extinction.

This emphasis on memory tries to avoid not only technically produced images and surface-only characters but also the death of the narrator, a theme that had been given an ironic treatment in Machado de Assis's last novels: both Brás Cubas (in *Memórias Póstumas de Brás Cubas*) and the conselheiro Aires (in *Memorial de Aires*) are dead narrators. In his speech Brás Cubas—not an author who happens to be dead, but rather a dead man who happens to write, as he describes himself—makes no attempt to stress his personal uniqueness; on the contrary, his speech is humorously duplicated in that of Quincas Borba and in countless digressions and interruptions.[6] As Roberto Schwarz has observed, what characterizes the late novels of Machado de Assis is precisely this "volubility": "That is, the narrator constantly denies his own identification with the position he occupied in the previous sentence, paragraph, chapter, or episode. . . . It is a sort of permanent de-identification" (Schwarz 1982: 316).

Attempts at de-identification are handled more (*Madame Pommery*) or less (*O professor Jeremias*) effectively by authors of the period, but most of the time they are simply ignored in these journeys into memory, concerned as they are with restoring the past rather than reflecting on alternative ways of narrating that can be constructed in (amorous or warlike) confrontation with this double landscape of things and images that has become a part of everyday experience.

This, however, is not true of Raul Pompéia's *O Ateneu*—published around the same time as Machado de Assis's mature works—or of Hilário Tácito's *Madame Pommery*. In *O Ateneu* there is an opposition between Sérgio the reminiscing narrator and Aristarco the sandwich man, which leads to the elaboration of a different diction, bordering on the essay, made up of Dr. Cláudio's speeches and comments on art, education, science, and literature, which produces two other kinds of tension in the novel. The first is an explicit tension between his speeches and conventional rhetoric. The second, which has to do with Pompéia's narrative style, is a tension between the text of memoirs and that of the essay. The narrator sometimes speaks from a seemingly safer place—past experience—and sometimes digresses into quasi-lectures that exploit the contrasts and clashes between his spectators. An example of this is Dr. Zé Lobo's vehement defense of institutions during Dr. Cláudio's first lecture.

In *Madame Pommery*, the narrative landscape is quite different. As a character, Madame Pommery is a sort of label; at the same time, several layers of digression are necessary to build this character and its fictional biography. Here the figure of the narrator is not established in opposition to this poster-like character, as was the case in *O Ateneu*, or in opposition to the fame that reveals subjectivity, as in *O professor Jeremias*. Toledo Malta, or "Hilário Tácito," works simultaneously with two dimensions: that of the all-surface character and that of an in-depth narrative. Thus there is a double landscape, between digression and a narrator who defines himself by his own reflexive ability, on the one hand, and the surface of a label, a character who is depersonalized as a brand of champagne, on the other.

In Toledo Malta's novel, the contrast is not between fiction and memory but between fiction and essay. The reference to Montaigne near the beginning of the book is not gratuitous; for those initial pages describe the characteristic narrative method of *Madame Pommery*: narration by digression and the creation of a fictional reader with whom a continuous dialogue takes place.

Here is a typical passage in which the reader is directly addressed:

Let there be no doubt about it: this is an honest book, a book written in good faith. I might well have given it Montaigne's epigraph: *C'est icy un livre de bonne foy, lecteur.* If I did not do it, it was because I did not want to, because from the outset I knew this quotation should turn up later, and I abhor repeating what I have said before. If, however, the reader should find it convenient or laudable, let him place this inscription right on the title page, on the condition that he will copy it very carefully, without changing the spelling. (Tácito 1977: 14)

The reflexive meanderings that make up the novel are clearly stated. It is made no less clear that if the figure of the narrator is stressed it is not in contrast with the caricature-like characters that frequent the Paradis Retrouvé, the brothel owned by the main character, or the advertisement figure of Madame Pommery herself. Here the affirmation of the narrator is accomplished by two complementary processes: there is a succession of digressions that are so interwoven into the fragile threads of the narrative that the narrative itself remains suspended, like the numerous digressions and odd comments; and there is also the fictionalization of another subjectivity that seems to affirm that of the narrator: the reader's. The reader is sometimes promised a linear narrative; sometimes his perspicacity is doubted; and sometimes he is asked to fill in gaps. But at all times a possible narrative pact is represented, though it must be readjusted now and then. Thus at one point the narrator gives the reader "a light tap on the shoulder" and asks him, at a moment when his thoughts are elsewhere: "Will you please do me a favor, sir? I owe you a couple of words." And after the reader throws away his cigarette and turns his attention to him, somewhat startled, the narrator says:

I propose to you, from the outset, a sort of mutual agreement. I request, I demand complete freedom to write according to my system and after my manner. The reader, whenever he does not feel he wishes to follow me in all these marginal ramblings, may simply leave me to pursue them on my own and follow the straight and narrow path of the narrative. And I assure the reader that we shall always meet again on the main road, after a brief separation. (Tácito 1977: 39–40)

But just as he proposes this pact, he comments ironically: "To walk about a garden without regarding the flowers?" (p. 41). For the life of Madame Pommery is relatively humdrum: she cheats on her father, a Polish Jew, and runs away from home; she opens her establishment in São Paulo by mere chance; she has three suitors (Pinto Gouveia, Dr. Mangancha, and Romeu de Camarinhas); her Paradis Retrouvé becomes amazingly successful; and she finally retires. Her entire career is just another example of what Paes calls "love-nest literature."[7] But what is told here is not just the story of Pomerikowsky. There is also a different story, with two main characters: an essayist-narrator and a reader to whom a number of pacts are offered but necessarily maintained in an undecided state, subject to the meanderings and digressions of the voluble narrator.

Thus the suggestion that the reader stick to the narrative line is only a sort of trick, a rhetorical introduction to a presentation of the opposite idea:

Nevertheless, I shall ever repeat, to whomever be wont to skip my much-maligned digressions, that they are the very soul and pith of this story, and one of the subtlest creations of human wit, ever since stories first came to be written in this world. (Tácito 1977: 40)

It is by means of digressions, then, that the narrator presents his self-portrait. And Tácito not only disowns any pretension to memoirs but ironizes the very idea of such a thing:

It is in the interest of this story to describe the general aspect of São Paulo when the city was first confronted with Mme. Pommery . . . .
. . . .
. . . .
... At this point it is only natural that my pen should tremble a little, dotting the page with suspension points that symbolize the winged leaps my mind takes on the road of time, back to that age, so highly regarded by poets, at which I was nauseated by my first cigarettes and felt the consequences of my first few bites into the forbidden fruit—more often than not, rotten. (Tácito 1977: 19)

The text refuses to allow personal memories any sort of aura. To the narrator of *Madame Pommery*, memory is an object of fun; he represents it as suspension points, humorously graphic gaps, instead of setting it in an ennobling frame, as is common in most memorialistic prose of the period.

Nothing could be more different from these sarcastic pokes at the past than the respectful elevation of memory by Camilo, in Gonzaga Duque Estrada's *Mocidade Morta*. To Camilo, memory is the mainspring of the "perception of the Self" (Estrada 1971: 194), and the inspiration for a "tormented prose":

The painful, painstaking, reminiscing digression into the Past he had indulged in, exhuming sorrows, resurrecting bygone times, had excited the intricate filigree of his nervous system, predisposing him to work neverendingly on his tormented sentences, consubstantiating the heteristic irregularity into the synthetic fabric of original pages, with the subtle penetration of self-scrutiny. He rose, like a sleep-walker, oblivious of himself, and walked inside. His steps died off in the distance ... (Estrada 1971: 195)

From the "winged leaps" of the narrator of *Madame Pommery* to Camilo's "tormented sentences," the distance is that which separates a text where the narrator is constructed through reflection and one where characters are defined by a subjectivity conceived as unique innerness. Thus the phrase "walked inside" in the passage above may be taken quite literally—first, because reminiscence functions as a way of direct access to one's own "Self," or "innerness"; second, because in the passage quoted Camilo is actually walking into the house in order to write. The strengthening of this "reserved space of subjectivity" is seen as a necessary condition for literary creation.

In the case of *Mocidade morta*, the narrative at times drifts into reflections on visual art, but this is not the novel's major point; affirmation, not reflection, is the goal. The book is a roman à clef about the Brazilian art milieu, but it also carefully constructs a subjectivity that thinks of itself as absolutely unique: Camilo's. This psychological and referential affirmation is akin to Coelho Neto's "odyssey of one's own youth," a project carried out in *A conquista*; and it is quite the opposite of *Madame Pommery*, where the narrator, Toledo Malta, purposely plays with the author's name ("Hilário Tácito") and where all characters, including the narrator, are presented as elements constructed by the narrative itself, as "fictional things." The protagonist herself is no exception:

Does Mme. Pommery actually exist, in flesh and blood? Here is a tricky question, one that, were I to avoid tackling it head on, might well mislead posterity into a fundamental, colossal blunder. Mme. Pommery might dwindle into a mere symbol, and my true story into no more than a novel, or even less than that. And why should not this novel turn out to be as immortal as, well, maybe not the *Aeneid* or the *Lusiads*, but as Rabelais or Brantôme?

So let Mme. Pommery be a symbol, if you will; I cannot forbid that. But, for the sake of truth, that eternally intangible substance, let us establish one point: That Mme. Pommery is alive and breathing, as truly as I, who write, and you, who read me, only much more voracious and longer of breath. (Tácito 1977: 29–30)

Even though he pretends to be writing a chronicle and he praises "true stories," Toledo Malta is derisive about the idea of truth as it relates to fiction prose. This is given an ironic turn when he establishes the "reality" of Pommery on the basis of an unexpected trick of analogical sleight-of-hand: her reality is founded on that of the narrator and that of the reader. In this way he makes it clear that the effect of verisimilitude is only the consequence of another pact. At the same time he indicates that the opening question in the passage might well be asked of other beings—the narrator, or even the seemingly safe reader, who could suddenly be faced with such a question as "Does the reader actually exist, in flesh and blood?"

Thus, having attributed an imaginary identity to the narrator ("Hilário Tácito") as well as to Mme. Pommery, the heroine whose name comes from a champagne label, the text creates another zone of undecidedness between this fictional reader, who is constantly mentioned, and the book's potential public. This zone of undecidedness, like the suspension points that ironically stand for the narrator's "winged leaps" in time, seems to undermine the "frank and truthful" revelation of invented or recollected individuals, and of intimate reminiscences of individuals or a whole generation. For if reader and narrator are as "real"—which is to say, as "literary"—as Pomerikowsky, clearly the book cannot be taken to reinforce the narrator's voice by giving the text the status of an essay, by restoring subjectivities lost or questioned by a burgeoning world of images and by the new technical landscape then taking shape in Brazil.

Thus the book's purpose is not to reaffirm truths or intimacies but to strengthen the figure of the narrator only in his literary role, rather than as a hiding place for personal truths to be revealed through literature, or as a way of suggesting the existence of "profound" thoughts and private spheres in the authorial subject or his reader. Hilário Tácito, a pseudonymous author, plays simultaneously with digressions and labels, perspectives and linear surfaces. *Madame Pommery* dissolves nostalgia in suspension points; the very type used in printing is given a critical and narrative function. The novel looks techniques and brand names in the eye, and with its razor-sharp digressions it destroys the texts written under the sign of memory, whose only resources are the exaggerated exhibition of "personalities" and the obsessive desire to substantiate the sincerity of the narrator and the truth of the narrative.

This ironic stance toward memoirs seems to anticipate the sharper sarcasm of Oswald de Andrade's *João Miramar*. Though an almost isolated attitude in the early decades of the century, it was to be inevitably reinforced by the changes in forms of perception and by the dawning of a new technological horizon. So it is that even texts that attempt to underscore cohesive individualities, such as Joaquim Nabuco's *Minha formação* (1900), are sometimes invaded by photographic procedures, snapshots, and stereotypes, which indirectly constrain the personalized flow of memory. A good example is found in "Massangana":

I have often sailed the sea, but whenever I try to recall it, nearly every time I find before my eyes, in a frozen instant, the first wave that ever rose before me, green and transparent as an emerald screen, one day when, having crossed a wide coconut grove behind the fishermen's huts, I found myself at water's edge and had the sudden, flashing revelation of a watery, moving land ... It was this wave, graven on the most sensitive plate of my childish Kodak, that became for me the eternal stereotype of the sea. (Nabuco 1934: 183)

Thus, when he tries to express one of the four or five early impressions that left an indelible mark on him, Nabuco suddenly resorts to "Kodak" and "stereotype." This suggests that even in those texts where subjectivities are amplified by memory and narrate themselves endlessly, in opposition to the all-surface characters of other texts, some industrial product or artifact somehow makes an appearance, as if this were inevitable, and traces of technology were to be found even where least expected. The technological landscape, from the poster and the printed page, seems to cast an unsympathetic eye on this flow of memories, subjectivities, and interiors.

A Character Seen Through a Windowpane

But lyrical, intimate Kodaks were not quite the rule in the Brazilian fiction of the period. They surface in only a few texts, and sometimes unintentionally. In fact, attempts to combine lyrical subjects and modern artifacts, inner feelings and snapshots, were not at all common. In poetry, too, what predominated were careful contrasts and disguises. The goal was to set up literary "craftsmanship" against colloquial language, prosaism, the hybridism of journalistic text, the threats to the breakdown of the boundaries and the hierarchical relations between the genres; and also to emphasize subjectivities in opposition to reduplications and standardizations, to affirm a timeless conception of literature against the changes it was already experiencing. For if since the late nineteenth century Brazilian poetry had been flirting with advertising, *crônicas*, snapshots, and movie subtitles, other kinds of dialogue went on with the technical landscape as well. These dialogues betrayed a clear rejection of this new landscape and of the kind of poetry that had no qualms about embracing it.

Literature then brought into being a new landscape, neither nature nor world of images. It is a changing landscape, sometimes entirely subjective, sometimes both antinature and antitechnology, sometimes subjected to a violent displacement in space and time, away from everyday scenery. Interiors, "pure artifacts," historical tableaux: such is the reaction against deindividualization; the dissemination of new machinery; the domination of advertising, the instant, and speed; the patterns, paces, and forms of industrial production.

Thus Camilo, in *Mocidade morta*, walks inside when he resolves to write—that is, withdraws into his house and into whatever hideouts are contained in his tormented subjectivity. This movement is the opposite of that of the advertising that dominated urban life at the turn of the century. "Regard the newspapers and magazines. They are filled with photogravures and names—names and faces, many names and many faces!" observed João do Rio (1910: 98). To be seen was all-important, as was to seem unique, even if subjected to the standardization of photography and journalistic profiling. And it made little difference whether one was seen as a socialite, a man of letters, or a criminal. What really counted was the sight of a changing urban scenery, photographs in the magazines, recognizable and individualized shapes for brands and models.

Mass production and new techniques of reproduction were accompanied by an obsessive desire for uniqueness. It is at this point that advertising and interiors, posters and secrets intersect: Nabuco's childhood memories suddenly turn into snapshots. And those who reject illustrations and ads do so in the name of a different way of making themselves known, in function of a lyrical self that elevates itself by means of confessions and unique traces.

This is the reason behind the proliferation of interiors that characterized Brazilian poetry of the early twentieth century. True, this preference cannot be explained solely in terms of a contrast between the lyricism of privacy and the world of advertising. It is not only as a reaction against the deindividualization posed by industrial reproduction that we can understand the vogue for "penumbrist interiors" of the 1910's and 1920's. The exacerbated and rhetorical subjectivity and the lachrymose poetry that were dominant in Brazilian Romanticism certainly had a decisive influence on this defense of a cohesive, all-powerful lyrical self through the affirmation of the private. But the rising technological world was clearly the driving force behind this poetry of interiors.

It is as though, in this changing setting, the poet, aware that it would be impossible to escape it entirely, opted for a place that was neither entirely integrated into the landscape nor completely outside it, at a certain remove from the street but facing it, far enough to lessen the sounds and sights of the outside world. An intermediate position functioning as a filter to domesticate the shock of modernization, the window was one of the favorite vantage points of the penumbrista poetry of the period.

In 1926, Kandinsky wrote, in *Point and Line to Plane*: "The street may be observed through the window pane, causing its noises to become diminished, its movements ghostly, and the street itself, seen through the transparent but hard and firm pane, to appear as a separate organism, pulsating 'out there' " (Kandinsky 1994: 532). This "beyond" is characteristically described in Ribeiro Couto's "Carícia," the first two stanzas of which are translated below:

> Every sound that, from outside,
> enters the sickroom where I lie
> loses some of its power:
> it comes muted, subdued ...
>
> Cries of street vendors, laughter,
> hammers on anvils—everything
> acquires blurred edges,
> is muffled in velvet.
>
> (Couto 1960: 49)

What comes from outside are the cries of vendors, laughter, singing, various city noises. But as they seep into the room they suffer inevitable changes. "Things coming from outside are *filtered* and *adapted* to the indoor environment," observes Goldstein (1983: 83) in her analysis of the poem.[8] And they all take on a certain "phantom" quality: noises are "muffled in velvet." They are neither entirely lost nor experienced in full; everything is diluted in the process of passing through the window, and the sickroom walls act as mufflers, letting in the various sounds of the workaday world without causing any discomfort.

The window is also the place where perception is attuned to the new images and the frantic pace of the streets. In Guilherme de Almeida's "Alma triste da rua," for instance, we read:

> It is from this window, up above,
> that my soul, little by little, grows used
> to feeling, on the sidewalks and the road,
> the sad soul of the street.
>
> (Almeida 1929: 25–27)

Or in Ribeiro Couto's poem—significantly titled "Interiores"—in which the image of seeing the world at a distance from one's bedroom window reappears:

> From my second-floor window
> I see, in this square full of trees,
> the lighted windows around.
> And there's always a newspaper and a lamp
> in the circumspect silence of the room.
>
> (Couto 1960: 61)

The world outside is like a landscape framed by the inner landscape of the bedroom. At times, innerness is attributed even to the outside world:

Guilherme de Almeida speaks of "the sad soul of the street," while the title of one of João do Rio's books is "The enchanting soul of the streets." Other interiors, other privacies, are seen as a horizon of circumspect windows, from the vantage point of another window, somewhat less circumspect, from which everything is "muffled in velvet."

And if from these "interiors" of Ribeiro Couto and Guilherme de Almeida there is at least a window opening out to other similar windows or to the street, sometimes these "figurations of privacy"[9] point to exclusive places, nooks secluded from the world, hideaways for individuality.

In *Histórias do meu casal* (1906), Mário Pederneiras asks, in "Vida simples":

> For my contemplative
> And sentimental soul,
> What spot could be better
> Than this sweet refuge of mine?
> (Pederneiras 1958: 49)

The question, merely rhetorical, actually involves the affirmation of complete privacy. The poet seems to be saying that it is only away from the life of the streets, of the public sphere, that the "real self" is to be found. A similar statement about "solitary souls" and the "tyrannies of inwardness" appears in Olegário Mariano's "Silêncio," included in *Evangelho da sombra e do silêncio* (1912), which presents another depiction of an exclusive privacy:

> In search of happiness, I fled the World,
> The commercial noises of this city.
> And here, in this remote, deserted place,
> Where life is sweet and quiet,
> I see in all their fullness
> My oldest, fondest dreams of happiness.
> (Mariano 1911–12: poem no. 17)

In this case, the praise of privacy is accompanied by an explicit refusal of the "commercial noises" of the city, as if not even the windowpanes and walls of a room facing the street were enough to filter out its sundry sounds and sights. It is worth underscoring, however, that the lyrical subject rejects a particular kind of sound: the "commercial noises" of the city. The private is affirmed as a sort of hiding place away from the marketplace, a protection from the fact that professionalization and industrial reproduction have suddenly threatened to transform literature into a consumer commodity or a source of income like any other.

Thus interiors are seen as the last refuges of the "aura," both for literary production and for producers of literature. In these havens, profundities and personalities can be protected from turning into caricatures or advertisements, from finding themselves reduced to the condition of pure surfaces, in spite of all the fictionalized subjectivities and journeys into the "depths" of the mind. This seems to be the point of a well-known sonnet by Augusto dos Anjos, "O morcego," in which allegory is a device for the affirmation of the self and consciousness. The setting is a bedroom; the situation is the sudden irruption of a bat, which refuses to go away:

> "I'll have another wall put up," I say.
> I stand up, trembling. I lock the door,
> Gaze at the ceiling. And I see it still,
> Like a round eye, right above my hammock!
>
> I grab a stick. I stretch my arm. I barely
> Touch it. My soul is concentrated. What womb
> Could have borne such horrid offspring?!
>
> The Human Conscience is such a bat!
> However hard we try, at night it steals
> Imperceptibly into our room!
>
> (Anjos 1971: 59)

As the new urban and industrial façade comes into sharper focus, interior landscapes of privacy multiply. The more time is perceived as an instant, the more histories and memoirs are written. Thus we may understand this multiplicity of interiors, these supposedly in-depth, in-perspective portraits of the lyrical subject, as, at least in part, oblique responses to the new technological world that dawned in the late nineteenth century.

The creation of interiors and windows points to a marked singularization of characters, places, and consciousnesses. But some windows, such as the ones in Couto's "Interiores," are ironically melancholy: identical, they suggest personalized private spaces which in fact are exactly alike in their silence, their lighted lamps, their abandoned newspapers, and their circumspection. And, indiscreetly, they may also be seen as forming a series of windows, each of which looks out onto other privacies. But other windows are attempted as well, windows that face other possible havens for subjectivity. Dr. Félix in *Vida ociosa* suggests as much when, taking an early morning walk to Old Man Próspero's farm, he reflects: "At such times one's soul is disturbed; *someone* inside me leans out of the window of the past and casts a nostalgic eye on something I cannot quite make out" (Rangel n.d.: 19).

As in memoirs, in Brazilian poetry from the turn of the century to the 1920's there are plenty of "windows onto the past"—and not just the past. At times, they provide a glimpse of the world of legend, as in Bilac's "Lendo a Ilíada," "Diziam que … ," or "A morte to Tapir"; or else a view of the nation's glory, as in "O caçador de esmeraldas," also by Bilac, the period's most representative poet—not for nothing did 104 of the 124 writers polled by the magazine *Fon-Fon* choose him as the "Prince of Brazilian Poetry" in 1913. There were also archaeological journeys, as in Alberto de Oliveira's "Vaso grego." Most often, there was the nostalgic trip down the road of individual memory, like the one described in terms of an imaginary auditory impression in Olegário Mariano's "Silêncio," the last stanza of which is:

> I remember … I remember … Bygone time
> As it flowed past, almost unheeded,
> Is like a sound most faint
> Still lingering in my ear.
> (Mariano 1911–12: poem no. 17)

However, like the allegorical and historical paintings that came to predominate in Brazilian academic painting after the 1850's, the temporal shifts in poetry have more to do with different thematic fields than with different techniques in the treatment of various chronological segments. True, in personal reminiscences, in "poetical interiors"—as in the domestic scenes of Rafael Frederico, a good painter of interiors of this period— or in the luminous interiors of Georgina de Albuquerque, the "mannerisms" are fewer, the setting is sparser, ordinary, and the tone is much more colloquial than in the historical or mythological works of Bilac or Alberto de Oliveira, for instance. In the case of these two poets, there are shifts either to the remote past, for the description of patriotic events, or to mythological time, and the literary technique remains basically the same.

Words, rhymes, and impressive settings combined to result in the creation of an alternative world, outside of history or of any recognizable geography. This occurred even in the poetical representation of historical facts or personages known to all; these were also submitted to the same process of artisanal "petrification" that the Parnassians valued so highly.

The actual referents, if any, were of little relevance; artificial landscapes and literary constructions were consciously used here.[10] They were not intended to stand for any actual—natural or technological—landscapes. The idea was to produce autonomous poetical objects, unconcerned with mediations and referents, in clear contrast with modern techniques of dissemination and reproduction of images and sounds: "pure artifact"—to use the term with which Antonio Candido defined the dominant poetical project during the Parnassian-symbolist period in Brazil[11]—in opposition to the "industrial artifacts" that became increasingly widespread after the 1880's.

Poetical craftsmanship vs. industrial reproduction; private interiors vs. technological landscapes; rhetorical profundities vs. all-surface characters; selves vs. caricatures: these oppositions reveal a somewhat desperate effort to reinvent objects and characters that are subject to the danger of being diluted at any moment. The same applies to the sacralizing concept of art, to the hideaways of subjectivity and single experiences, to the possibility of escaping the world of advertising and building a personality that was definitely not all surface.

These extreme contrasts bring to mind a comment by Jean Baudrillard concerning a more recent period, but which applies equally to the striving for singularization that is characteristic of both the fin-de-siècle "pure artifact" poetry and the poetry of "interiors" of the first few decades of the twentieth century. Referring to the obsession with *personalization* in industrial society—which is no less typical of the "poetical interiors" we have been examining—Baudrillard writes:

All that this rhetoric says, in its struggle with the impossibility of saying it, is precisely *that there is nobody*, whether the "person" as an absolute value, with irreducible traits and specific weight, forged by the Western tradition as the organizing myth of the subject, endowed with passions, will, and character, or . . . its banality; this person is absent, has been banished from our functional universe. And it is this absent person, this lost instance, that must be "personalized." (Baudrillard 75: 133)

But interiors were not the only devices resorted to in the quest for personalization. There were other tricks as well. A rather clever one was the attempt to strengthen the lyrical self "photographically," as it were, by bringing together lyricism and technique. An example of this is found in the poem "Autofotografia," by the Curitiba poet Adolfo Werneck, included in *Bizarrias* (1908), where the reader is invited to a curious journey into a subjectivity converted into a Sunday landscape. It is a gray, sunless Sunday, an idea that provides the basis for the analogy between poet and landscape that is repeated throughout the sonnet:

> The sky laughs not, the sky is sad, it is
> Rather like me, who dream ominous dreams,
> Ill forebodings, things that haunt
> The mind of an exhausted invalid.
>
> O melancholy Sunday!
> No laughing, no songs, not a whit
> Of joy … Just as gloomy
>
> Am I, and for those who know me not,
> Seeing such a day is much the same
> As looking at a portrait of me.
>
> (Quoted in Muricy 1973, 2: 803–4)

It is a rather artless poem, of naive self-revelation, with far too many "I"s and "me"s for a poem whose title already means "Self-photography." And the double analogy suggested—between lyrical self and sunless Sunday on the one hand, and poem and photographic image on the other—seems weak at both ends. The first analogy is too obvious and does not leave the reader any possibilities of finding unsuspected parallels between the interior scene and the Sunday landscape; the analogy is too explicit; the similarity is presupposed rather than established by the imagery. The same goes for the second analogy, with photography; the similarity with technically produced images alluded to in the title is simply mentioned gratuitously, no effort being made by the poet to apply photographic devices to his literary technique. This was to happen only later, in Mário de Andrade's *Pauhcéia desvairada* (Hallucinated city, 1922)—one thinks of the "Paisagens" series, particularly number 3—and in Oswald de Andrade's systematic use of montage and texts in series.

"In my opinion, to write modern art never means to represent modern life through its externals: automobiles, movies, asphalt," wrote Mário de Andrade in his preface to *Pauhcéia desvairada* (1968: 16). But the earliest attempts to approach this changing landscape, characterized not by displacement but by bedazzlement or explicit rejection, generally assumed the form of "faithful" imitation, not of the new processes available but of this or that sign of modernization. It was as if the representation of modernity made the work modern; or, in the case of "Autofotografia," as if it were enough to refer to the world of technology, in a text marked by melancholy subjectivism, to disguise its antiquarian nature; as if a photograph of a ruin could restore it.

However, not all attempts to combine the expression and affirmation of subjectivity with modern artifacts were reduced to mentioning them in a title. In his "Telefone," included in *Era uma vez* . . . (1922), for instance, Guilherme de Almeida tried—primarily by means of layout and punctuation—to syncopate the poem, in analogy with the unfinished and fragmented speech characteristic of telephone conversation. This device might have led him to find unexpected connections, to make the poetic text truly dialogic; but this he fails to do. "Telefone" turns out to be one more poem in which the poetic voice is subjective and unique, even though supposedly engaged in a dialogue, and seems to repeat, with no significant interruptions, the old images and rhetorical formulas of amorous language. Once again the reference to technology is a mere façade, which fails to affect poetic technique in any unexpected way. Here is a translation of the poem:

> Hello! It's me . . .
>   Good morning!
>   I'm all right; how about you?
> You've read my poem? Yes?
>   Indiscreet? But why?
> People will know? But that is just
> what I want . . .
>   Why not? I want everyone
> to envy me.
>   But I do want them
> to know about it all!
>   Of course: where love is concerned
> indiscretion means vanity . . .
>   I wouldn't
> dare? In front of everyone? You bet
> I would! I wouldn't say it? Want to hear me
>   say it? With pleasure . . .
> Listen!
>   I can't, I'm not alone here, I'd be overheard . . .

In "Telefone," the telephone acts as a modern *referendum* in a monologue made up of short sentences, filled with exclamations points, question marks, and suspension points. Another attempt—a slightly more daring one—to incorporate city noises into the text is a 1920 prose piece—"Um prego! Mais outro prego! . . . " by Adelino Magalhães. In a mixture of interior monologue and delirium caused by the Spanish flu, a man builds a coffin for his dead daughter, and as he works all the sounds of the street—of the vehicles, passersby, and buildings—are painfully metamorphosed by his despair and his fever.

When he hears "the lumbering sound of a truck over the paving stones," he describes it as "hair-raisingly funereal."[12] When the clock strikes, it sounds "ill or forlorn, or full of wintry yearning." When the newsboy yells "The *News*! More scandals in the Santa Casa!,"[13] he feels "a tremor in his nerves," and the sound seems to him to announce "a tune different from the usual one: diseased, gloomy, frightened" (Muricy 1973: 937). Even the sound of a streetcar, which at first "seemed to give him the unexpected impression of ordinariness," soon gives way to the unpleasant scene of the expulsion of a woman who was trying to travel with a live hen in a basket. "There was a fright in each thing" is how the character sums it all up.

Under the impact of the epidemic, of the despair caused by his own sickness and the death of his child, the entire city landscape is inexorably changed. Two cities, radically different, come to his mind. The first is "gay," "fatuous," "radiant":

The streetcars and automobiles and façades and all men and things seemed to smile, disdainfully, and rush about ... immune to the malady, vaccinated against the malady, by the pride of being the City, untouchable and privileged! (Muricy 1973: 933)

The second version is a city seen from the viewpoint of desolation:

Oh! the same city he was to see weeks later in a deathly guise of devastation, tattered with dirty dead leaves, rags, organic wastes, in the slovenly litter of its silent streets, where only the odd vehicle looms every now and then, often with funereal intent, frightening the few gaunt and distraught passersby, who move like stealthy shadows! (P. 933)

This landscape of devastation is gradually combined with the image of the other city, transforming it almost completely, so that the earlier setting turns into a projection of individual despair. The outside world is personalized little by little, taking the form of a suffering, delirious subjectivity. The city takes on the likeness of a feverish self.

But this symbiotic combination between the character and the city façade does not carry any radical implications. For it is all justified by the delirium. The apparently chaotic distortions in the perception of city sights and sounds have a medical explanation. The deformations are controlled by a subjectivity that is never questioned by the narrative. Its delirious state is known, but the image world is transformed according to its own laws, which are powerful but ephemeral. Nowhere is it indicated that these laws of symbiosis and metamorphosis may indeed generate a different perception of the city and everyday life. These uncanny nexuses exist only as consequences of delirium, as a possibility of affirmation— even if in a context of disease—of an absolutely individual viewpoint, from which the setting of everyday life is regarded and this subject in agony is singularized as the axis of the transformations and meanings involved in Adelino Magalhães's text.

But these excursions into interiors and subjectivities turn increasingly cruel. Examples are Oswald de Andrade's "Meus oito anos," a parody of a well-known sentimental poem by Casimiro de Abreu, included in "Primeiro caderno de poesia do aluno Oswald de Andrade" (1927), and Mário de Andrade's "A escrivaninha," included in *Losango cáqui* (1926), three stanzas of which are translated below:

> Father and his Jewish nose …
> I lived almost soundlessly.
> Dumas Terrail Zola in secret,
> If he finds out … My father? My God?
>
> Two persons in a single terror.
> My furtive fourteen years of age:
> Trashy readings, ugly vices,
> So much worthless past! …
>
> Then life taught me
> Life. Father died. When
> I saw I was an orphan, in tears,
> My misery was over …
>   (Andrade 1966b: 86–87)

"My father? My God?" The questions, one immediately following the other, suggest a relentless analogy, and are accompanied by a wholly negative view of the past—"worthless"—and of the image of the father, synonymous with misery and terror. Here there are no tender family ties as in Adelino Magalhaes's delirious monologue. In this poem by Mário de Andrade, "leaning out of the window of the past" is not a way of reviving the past or of inventing a golden age of childhood, but rather a way of killing the past.

Such a murder is perpetrated in only two lines by Oswald de Andrade in one of his instant poems, "Velhice" (Old age):

> Little grandson dropped the spectacles
> Into the toilet
>
> (Andrade 1974: 99)

Here the past is not even individualized: the family snapshot is ironically impersonal. There is no tenderness directed at old age, or at the world in general, or at the experiences of any ancestral generation. In one and the same gesture, the text desacralizes the traditional concept of poetry (here submitted to a telegraphic synthesis), the domestic scene, the seductiveness of lifeless objects ("in the toilet"), and family albums. "Because affects should be like wings that brush over one's soul or skin" (Campos 1985: 166–67), as Kilkerry said of the "modern 'polis'" in 1913, perhaps such a murder was already predictable. The more difficult target was different: subjectivity itself, a relic to be all the more protected because it seemed to be constantly under threat.

To fragment the image of the world is one thing; to risk an all-powerful *ego scriptor* is something quite different. For this implies, if nothing else, undermining a narrow but dominant conception of lyricism as the expression of an "uncommon" craftsmanship or of a self that unceasingly confesses or projects itself onto the most varied objects, themes, and situations. Once this self—on which meanings are usually woven in the poem—is lost, it becomes necessary to develop new ways of constructing meaning and to test ironic forms of impersonality, multiplying masks and allowing the juxtaposition or confrontation of various types of discourses and images, in hitherto unforeseen montages.

This brings about a series of attacks on conventional conceptions of poetry. There are, for instance, the many parodies of poetry as historical description in Oswald de Andrade's *Pau-Brasil* (1925). And in "música de manivela," a poem from the same book, an advertisement invades what seemed to be a depiction of a scene of domestic privacy:

> Sit before the phonograph
> And forget life's vicissitudes
> In the hard toil of each day
> No one with any self-respect
> Should neglect the pleasures of the soul
>
> Phonograph records all prices
>
> (Andrade 1974: 61–62)

The poem is in the imperative mood, as if the whole text were a hard-sell effort. The phrases are half mechanical, like recordings, automatic repetitions of a memorized text. The poem has no clear subject or interlocutors; it is close to being an "industrial product." It turns a devastating eye to the sort of poetry that seeks profundity and the soul; in "música de manivela" pleasure and happiness are things that can be bought in any department store, for "all prices."

This is the very opposite of the tormented doubts expressed by Raimundo Correa, for instance, in "Fetichismo":

> It is in vain, O Man, you ask
> Of ruthless shades: "In what heaven
> Does God dwell? Where is this region drenched
> In blessed light, home of the just and faithful?"
>
> In vain your shaking hands do grope
> Their way into the endless, empty night,
> Where horrid doubt cries and curses,
> And all is lamentation and gnashing of teeth ...
>
> (Correia 1922: 242–43)

Contrast this piece of metaphysical despair with this text from the "Postes da Light" section of *Pau-Brasil*:

> Happiness goes on foot
> On praça Antônio Prado
> It's 10 o'clock and blue
> Coffee is high like the skyscrapered morning
>
> Tietê Cigarettes
> Automobiles
> City without myths
>
> (Andrade 1974: 64)

One can hardly read "In what heaven does God dwell?" without a sense of irony after running into such a line as "Happiness goes on foot," or after seeing such high-sounding images as "life's vicissitudes" and "pleasures of the soul" being used to advertise phonograph records.

Even subjectivity and one's innermost desires, then, are turned into pictures at an exhibition. Two passages from *Memórias sentimentais de João Miramar* are particularly illustrative.

The first is the scene in which Miramar speaks of his passion for Gisella Doni.

Musicians walked in, and the first idle faces installed themselves in the back seats of the audience. I secretly desired Gisella.

Steps filled confused scales of flutes and affirmative violins. The audience was witness to my love. (Andrade 1975: 21)

It all takes place simultaneously: the revelation of love, the tuning-up of the orchestra, the arrival of the audience. These are pictures exhibited in nonhierarchical succession. Passion is just another object on show.

The second passage is also a "love story." But the love object is different: Miramar is marrying Célia. The wedding is all patterned on interior-decoration schemes, furniture, clothes, and holiday traveling appropriate to "a perfect life for a couple."

A crayon by a Parisian architect that we had seen before the wedding had inspired in us a desperate envy for a calm marital existence, complete with pajamas and bedside lamps, under the protection of the ancient gods of man. (Andrade 1975: 40)

Married life as a crayon drawing, or caricature: such is the treatment given to all passions, travels, and characters in the novel.

The narrator mocks himself in caricatures and memoirs—fragmented, unfinished memoirs that show no intention of vindicating the narrator and that seem to echo Machado de Assis's perverse use of the genre in his later works. If the death of the classical narrator is really inevitable, why not make fun of him? Why not dramatize the fragmentation that narrative is being subjected to—and exploit the comings and goings of a narrator who knows himself to be the prey, but who sometimes turns himself into the predator and puts on a different mask? These are the hints that Oswald de Andrade seem to take from Machado de Assis in *Memórias sentimentais de João Miramar* and *Serafim Ponte Grande*. And such issues, in a discussion of Oswald's prose, are necessarily associated with another—the relations between literature and technology, which had begun to become closer since the turn of the century but came to influence a significant part of Brazilian cultural production in a decisive way only in the 1920's.

"Once upon a time there was / The world" (Andrade 1974: 109). With this brief synthesis, Oswald seems to sum up—in one of the many possible readings of this poem, "Crônica,"—the changes experienced by Brazil between the 1890's and the 1920's. "Once upon a time there was / *A* world," one is tempted to rewrite the poem. For this was indeed a time of radical change in forms of perception, just as the period from the 1920's to the 1940's was to be: radio appeared in 1922 (but became important only in the 1930's), air transportation in 1927, assembly-line production of vehicles in 1920 (Ford) and 1925 (General Motors, twenty-five cars a day), and the use of electricity for sound recording in 1927. The next major changes were to come in 1950, with the introduction of television in São Paulo (it came to Rio in 1951), and in the 1970's, with the systematic use of video recording and color television, when Brazilian society underwent a decisive process of spectacularization.

But the period from the 1890's to the 1920's, when technology made its first inroads in Brazil, marks the beginning of the process. The first confrontations and earliest shocks caused by the large-scale dissemination and use of industrial processes and artifacts, the impact of this functional landscape and cultural production on literary technique—these were to be the hallmarks of this period, which is usually labeled pre-this or post-that in Brazilian history. It is a hesitant period, but it was to provide the earliest setting for the new landscape of machinery and serial images, and for the first literary responses to the new circumstances. As the poet might put it, once upon a time there was a mode of perception—or a definition of writing as craftsmanship. From that point on, literature was to be thought of as technique, and as just another element in a constantly changing landscape, where selves, ornamentation, and hiding places were to be replaced by a cinematograph of words.

Films and More Films

The phrase "cinematograph of words" is taken from a passage in João do Rio's introduction to his volume of 1908 *crônicas*, *Cinematógrafo*. But the image should not be understood in a univocal sense. For by the time Oswald de Andrade appropriated montage as a literary technique, movies were seen quite differently from the way they had been seen by João do Rio in 1909, or by Artur Azevedo who, in 1897, was optimistic about the new device's possibilities of recording not only views but also theatrical performances. And as one traces the changes in perceptions of the cinematograph one can also see how technology and its relations with literary production were perceived at different moments in the period.

From Artur Azevedo's cinematograph to João do Rio's cinematograph of words to Oswald de Andrade's montages, significant changes in perspective took place. The early view of the camera as basically a documentary device gave way to the notion that behind it there was the eye of the filmmaker, recording his "personal impressions" on film. By the 1920's the awareness had come that cinema had a language of its own, that rather than just reproduce images the camera produced them in accordance with a syntax and a logic of its own.

So it was that at first technology was merely mentioned in literary works, and technical devices made a cameo appearance here and there. But when the industrial logic and the specific language of the movies, photography, and photochemical printing methods were understood, then elaborations and critical appropriations of technical devices became more common.[14]

From mention to appropriation, then, was a continuous process, three moments of which I highlight with examples from three journalists: Artur Azevedo (two texts published in 1901 and 1906), João do Rio (1909) and Benjamin Costallat (1922).

Let us begin with Artur Azevedo's weekly drama column, published in the daily *A Notícia*. On September 12, 1901, after showering praise on Clara Della Guardia's performance in Giacose's *Come le foglie*, Azevedo expressed the desire "that it might be preserved forever by means of a cinematograph and a phonograph."[15] A few years later, on December 3, 1906, in a *crônica* published in *O País*, he describes in detail a private exhibition of Behring & Co.'s cinematograph:

The machine itself is not very much superior to others; but the films are, some of them amounting to veritable dramas, complete with exposition, catastrophe, and denouement.

One of these dramas, "The Deserter," is the story of an officer who falls in love with a music-hall singer and because of her steals money from the regiment safe, which incidentally was not at all well guarded. The spectator follows the story from the moment the two lovers first meet until the unfortunate young man's arrest, degradation, and suicide—he blows his brain out with a revolver, taken to his dungeon by a venerable old man, obviously his father.

Another drama, "Kidnappers," seems to be based on D'Ennery. The audience is offered the martyrdom of a boy stolen from his home in order to be exploited as a beggar by a horrid harridan very much like Frochard in "The Two Orphans." Such was the artistry of the performance that many wept.

Both when he suggests that Clara Della Guardia's performance be recorded and when he praises the exhibition at Behring & Co., Artur Azevedo is not really concerned with the cinematograph itself and its specific way of producing images, with the new medium and its "grammar," but rather with the sort of scenes that should be recorded on film.

He believed that what was important then was to emphasize the "artistic" and "emotional" effectiveness of filmed drama:

This proves that this remarkable apparatus can be applied to the art of drama. The people who appeared in those scenes are true artists, very accomplished in mime and facial expression. By means of the cinematograph, our grandchildren will be able to have an idea of who Sarah Bernhardt was—particularly if the phonograph is perfected in such a way that the two devices will complement each other.

To Azevedo, then, film's most important asset is its ability to record and reproduce at will such unrepeatable events as dramatic performances. And when he sees artistry in filmed images, the artistry is not exactly in the actual film but in the theatrical performance that is represented in the film medium. When he says that the cinematograph is a "remarkable apparatus," he is not thinking of the possibility of cinematic language; such a thing would be unthinkable to him. What is "remarkable" about film is its ability to represent other languages, to preserve "artistry" as it is manifested elsewhere. "By means of the cinematograph," he writes: and to him movies are just that, a neutral, chameleon-like means that can even take on the appearance of art, as long as it aims its lens at artistic scenes. The medium was perceived not in its own materiality, or as having its own language, but as a transparent conveyor of images, the quality of which alone determined the artistry of such exhibitions as the one Azevedo saw at Behring & Co.

Three years after this comment of Azevedo's was published in *O País*, João do Rio, in the introduction to his *Cinematógrafo*, underscored another aspect of film that he found of great importance. This was the fact that movies were very much influenced by the camera operator's personal choices and viewpoints:

Ultimately, the cinematograph is a series of stories and personal impressions of an operator in search of the "right moment"; it is the mark of his temperament in choosing a subject already prepared, and in looking for the positions from which to shoot. (Rio 1909: ix)

Thus, what determines João do Rio's evaluation is not exactly the "subject" but the perspective, the "right moment" chosen for the shooting; in other words, the take. But though João do Rio realizes that technique is not completely neutral, that it depends directly on the eye of the operator, this does not lead him to dwell too long on the possibility of a "cinematic language"; instead he focuses on the figure of the operator. Film is no longer a transparent conveyor of different views: it is a sort of moving diary of varied personal impressions, the self-portrait of a temperament. Chameleon-like, it takes on the contours of the operator's "personality." And what is emphasized is the medium's ability to capture the "romance of the operator's life," even if combined with "the labyrinth of facts, other people's lives, and fantasy," "caught up in the torrent of events" and characterized only by "a mid-way point of emotion."

Closer to the 1920's, when there was much more familiarity with the technological landscape—including the cinematograph itself—the situation was quite different. Let us examine one of the *crónicas* included in *Mutt, Jeff & Cia.* (1922), a book by Benjamin Costallat, a popular writer of the period. Though he seems to have somewhat mixed feelings about cinema ("beautiful in its achievements, grotesque in its essence," Costallat n.d.: 13), he was apparently aware that the "perfect illusion" projected onto the screen was related to the machine-specific language for reproducing moving images, with a syntax, forms of expression, and representation of its own. For all his misgivings, Costallat somehow realized that film has its own expressive and material resources that are not simply drawn from the subject being filmed or originated by the camera operator.

It is only natural, then, that Costallat should have focused on animated cartoons in his examination of film as language. He speaks of his "passion for Mutt and Jeff," in contrast to his rejection of many of the movies made at the time:

Animated caricatures, humor in motion, they achieve absolute novelty in cinema, being something altogether different from their flesh-and-blood colleagues. If their appearance is ridiculous, with their India-ink silhouettes, the observation behind them is true, and their psychology is precise. (Costallat n.d.: 13)

He sums up: "Mutt and Jeff are two types, two psychologies" (p. 14). Their ability to synthesize so much graphically and mechanically, plus the fact that they are explicitly *invented* characters, makes it possible to see cinema as not mere reproduction, but also invention. Of course, Costallat does not realize that Mutt and Jeff's "flesh-and-blood colleagues" are not exactly flesh and blood: they are technically produced images, just like Mutt and Jeff.

But this is not what is in question here. The point is that in the 1920's, especially because of animated cartoons, there was increasing awareness that films were the product of a set of "stylistic procedures." And after reflecting on these procedures and techniques, one finds it easier to elaborate on them or appropriate them in another form of expression. One's perception of film and technique changes, and instead of merely borrowing the odd term or image, one becomes able to use cinematic procedures in literature. This takes place in a doubly critical manner. First, there are always two targets involved: on the one hand, a literature of pure artifact and subjectivity wherein the "aura" took refuge; on the other, a standardization that was unable to reflect on its own development, as is typical of industrial methods of production. Second, in this critical flirtation between literature and technology, sometimes this supposedly pure art was desacralized, and sometimes technical resources were taken out of their original industrial context, so that their use was in some way made less automatic.

As Walter Benjamin observed about the use of the principle of interruption in Brecht's epic theater, "The superimposed element disrupts the context in which it is inserted" (Benjamin 1978: 234). That is why it is possible for an author like Oswald de Andrade to use montage both to corrode memoirs, naturalistic links, and verbal "richness" and to mock mechanistic and servile approaches to technical images. A perverse example of this is "Free-Will Mariquinha," an erotic mechanism sold to Serafim Ponte Grande by Major Duna Sabre in a Paris hotel room. Confused by all the wires, antennas, fuses, and "a racket of klaxons and several eye sockets," he gives up on Mariquinha and returns "to the arms of sleepless Joaninha" (Andrade 1975: 200).

Oswald de Andrade at times portrays artists in contexts that are equally ironic about technology. This seems to be his way of constantly reflecting on his own role, sometimes focusing on the way of perceiving or appropriating machinery and technical procedures or landscapes, sometimes caricaturing the purely superficial or excessively mimetic way of relating to such landscapes, typical in the productions of the period that attempt to show off their modernity.

At this point it would be instructive to contrast two similar scenes from radically different novels—Gonzaga Duque Estrada's *Mocidade morta* (1899) and Oswald de Andrade's *Serafim Ponte Grande* (finished in 1928). In both, a painter resorts to a photograph in order to paint a portrait of an absent person. But the aesthetic effect of one scene is quite different from the other's, a fact that points to different perceptions of the world of technology.

In *Mocidade morta*, Camilo, the critic, visits his friend, the painter Agrário, and finds him working on a portrait of a crooked businessman:

The painter was making a sketch, sometimes looking at the photograph for details, sometimes seeing it from a distance in order to have an idea of the whole, with quick pencil strokes, sometimes disjointed and confused, erased by a fingertip. The figure gradually came into view. It was like a faded memory being recalled, imperfect, vague, indefinite; in sfumato at first, then with sharper contours as the fusain insisted, thickening the lines, attempting minute details, highlighting points. (Estrada 1971: 202)

This mimetic relation with the photographic image is later reinforced by the behavior of Agrário's lover, Henriette, who, when the sketch was done, "rushed to the easel" and "stopped before the canvas, considering the sketch's likeness to the photographic image" (p. 203). In the novel, this situation indicates a certain "professionalization" of Agrário, not his "photographic" taste. But the very fact of Henriette's comparing the sketch and the photo, and the painter's melancholy feeling that the way of *imitatio* is inevitable, seem to point to an excessive respect for the "perfect illusion" made possible by technology. This is revealed no less clearly by the novel's anxious attempt to counterpose to it the subjectivity and the verbal ornamentation that are so important in it. It is as if Duque Estrada's narrative were meant to resist the new technology, even as Agrário's art had to succumb to it. Turn-of-the-century Brazil seems to hesitate before technology, not knowing whether to fear or admire it. In the case of Estrada's novel, technology is represented, but partly in order to keep it under surveillance and to counterpose to it a language intended as exclusively "literary," uncontaminated by industrial standards and processes.

The scene of the painting of Serafim's portrait, in Oswald de Andrade's novel, is quite different. After Serafim's death, his widow, Dona Lalá, and her new husband, Celestino Manso, build "in a suburb of Juqueri an asylum for the treatment of madness in all its forms" as a way to render a tribute to the dead man "in the philanthropic bronze of celebrations." Also, they commission "a painter from Europe to paint a photograph of the deceased in oils." They hand him "a Sunday snapshot" of Serafim with Pinto Calçudo and Birimba. But the result of his efforts, unlike Agrário's portrait of the businessman in *Mocidade morta*, does not please Serafim's family:

The painter worked patiently, honestly, furiously. But the portrait did not look like its subject. Dona Lalá thought he was thin, Beatriz thought he was fat, and Pombinho's filial opinion was that his eyebrows were full of bird shot.

The painter retouched his work. But Celestino thought there was a detail missing. The tip of his nose moved when he talked.

The painter, crazy as a syllogism, became the first inmate of the luxurious cells of the Serafim Asylum. (Andrade 1975: 257)

Unlike the scene in *Mocidade morta*, the criticisms made by Serafim's family make no reference to comparisons between the snapshot given to the painter and the portrait. Rather, they reflect impossible demands: his eyebrows were full of bird shot; the tip of his nose moved when he spoke. And the painter's attempt to make a precise reproduction of everything—everything in the photo, in the family's reminiscences—seems bound to fail. The author seems to be suggesting that the mimetic obsession is hopeless, and not only when the referent is a photograph. The painter's attempt to produce a painting containing no traces of invention lands him straight in the Serafim Asylum.

Oswald de Andrade, then, seems to be saying that the commitment to "faithful reproduction" at the expense of invention does not characterize technical processes of reproduction only. In the case of Serafim's portrait, for instance, it is the painter himself who tries desperately to establish a relation of continuity between portrait and "reality," between the work of art and the expectations of its restricted public. And this he attempts by means of the resources of painting, with no mechanical or technological means. Oswald de Andrade, in contrast, does not hesitate to juxtapose literary and technical landscapes and establish a mutually critical dialogue between them.

It is precisely this confrontation, this dialogue between montage and biography, quotation and caricature, fragment and snapshot, that turns out to be the real subject of the novel. The text, a story of travel, seems to make its double the ship *El Durasno*, which, at the end, amidst parodies of Camões, references to Havelock Ellis and Proust, radiograms, semaphores, and "the soft and geometrical copulation of engines," states its purpose to remain forever sailing. And, like the crew and passengers who will never return to land, the ship that cares only for the journey, not for the harbors, the novel, an ironic "antimechanism," is permanently calling its own bluff.

In a position close to paradox—like that suggested by Marcel Duchamp in "With My Tongue in My Cheek"—the travel book, as it tells Serafim's story, unceasingly exhibits its own narrative procedures, and in so doing points to the changes taking place in perceptions of literary activity. These changes would result in a weakening of literature's artisanal aspects and, in a context marked by the incorporation of modern artifacts into everyday landscapes, in literature's self-exposure as technique.

Avenida Central with pedestrians, automobiles, horse-drawn carriages, and bicycles. This avenue was the centerpiece of Rio's turn-of-the-century urban reform. (Arquivo Histórico da Fundação Casa de Rui Barbosa [FCRB])

Slum housing on rua do Senado, Rio de Janeiro. Photo by Augusto Malta, March 27, 1906. (Arquivo Malta, FCRB)

CINEMATOGRAPHO PARISIENSE – TAMBEM NA AVENIDA CENTRAL.

Cinematographo Parisiense, on avenida Central. (*Fon Fon*, year 1, no. 28, Oct. 19, 1907)

Interior of the Cinema Ideal, Rio de Janeiro. (*Revista da Semana*, Sept. 10, 1921)

Above: Illuminated dome of the Cinema Ideal. (*Revista da Semana*, Sept. 10, 1921)

Left: Cover of Benjamin Costallat's *Melle. Cinema: Novela de costumes do momento que passa* (Mlle. Cinéma: A novella of manners of the passing moment [Rio de Janeiro: Costallat & Miccolis Ed., 1923]), a Brazilian best-seller of the early 1900's.

Façade of Livraria e Editora Briguiet, Rio de Janeiro. (Arquivo Histórico, FCRB)

Page from *O Mequetrefe*, a Rio illustrated periodical, June 20, 1884, with an ad for Aluísio Azevedo's novel *Casa de pensão*, by Tipographia Militar de Santos & Cia. Parts of the book had been published in installments in the newspaper *Folha Nova*, from March to May 1883.

LITTERATURA

QUINCAS BORBA

LXXXIV

— E porque não ? perguntou uma voz, logo depois que o maior saiu.

Rubião, apavorado, olhou em volta de si; viu apenas o cachorro, parado, olhando para elle. Era tão absurdo crer que a pergunta viria do proprio Quincas Borba, — ou antes do outro Quincas Borba, cujo espirito estivesse no corpo deste, que o nosso amigo sorriu com desdem ; mas, ao mesmo tempo, executando o gesto do capitulo XLIX, estendeu a mão, e coçou amorosamente as orelhas e a nuca do cachorro, — acto proprio a dar satisfação ao possivel espirito do finado.

Era assim que o nosso amigo se desdobrava, sem publico, deante de si mesmo.

LXXXV

— E porque não ? repetiu a mesma voz mysteriosa.

Só agora advertiu Rubião que a bocca invisivel estava dentro d'elle ; a voz emergia das profundezas do inconsciente para interrogal-o. Sim, porque não havia de casar ? continuou andando e raciocinando, alvoroçado com essa ideia tão simples e tão complexa, tão facil e tão difficil. Casando, esquecia tudo. Mataria a paixão tardia e adultera que o in commodo aos poucas, seu esperança nem consolação. Demais, era a porta de um mysterio. Casar, sim, não havia outro recurso ; casar logo, casar bem. E Rubião ficou a andar de um lado para outro, sem calcar uma planta, uma flor, nada mais que a terra do chão; as pernas é que o levavam por si mesmas, direitas, lucidas, vagarosas, para que ficasse á cabeça tão somente a tarefa de pensar.

Boas pernas ! pernas amigas ! Muletas naturaes da alma ! Só pararam quando o creado veiu chamar o Rubião para jantar. Tambem era tempo ; a viagem tinha sido longa. E porque, segundo o velho Goethe, ha muito que contar depois de uma viagem, muito contaria o nosso amigo se pude se colligir todas as reminiscencias. Não podia; tal foi o turbilhão de cousas e pessoas que passaram por elle, vagamente, confusamente, que não distinguiria agora um só perfil, uma unica scena. Viu mãos de padre e hombros de

mulheres, ramalhetes de cravos brancos entremeados de hyssopo, olhos claros, olhos de todas as cores e tamanhos, bençãos, risos, lagrimas, carruagens, tudo de mistura, sem poder saber onde é que cada cousa principiava nem acabava.

Dias e dias vieram vindo e passando, sem adiantar nada ; mas a ideia conjugal persistia. Que elle é preciso deixar aqui bem claro, — a ideia de casar não era só isto, — nem tambem, como o nosso amigo presumia, — unicamente um modo de matar a paixão adultera. Era, antes de tudo, uma cousa obscura e inconsciente.

LXXXVI

Sim, leitor profundo. A vida de Rubião carecia de unidade. Sem o perceber, o que elle buscava no casamento era a unidade que a vida não tinha. Sentia-se disperso e confuso ; era como um morador de hospedaria, que passa, que está aqui dous dias, acolá quatro ; tem de visitar hoje um museo, amanhã uma ruina, para a semana outra cidade. Não convive, não mora ; fala no inglez, ao francez, ao italiano, ao allemão, ao russo, a todas as nações, de todas as maneiras, a pé, de carro, fumando, comendo.

Mas, ainda assim, a vida pode ter unidade, — ou

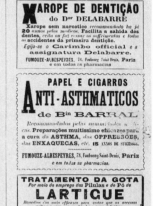

Page from *A Estação. Jornal ilustrado para a família* (year 17, no. 2), Jan. 31, 1888, with advertisements and part of Machado de Assis's novel *Quincas Borba* (Philosopher or dog). The journal published the novel and various stories by Machado de Assis in installments.

Photo of Lucy Penna Simões d'Oliveira wearing a costume that represents "the Press" at a children's ball in the Sport Club do Pará, on May 7, 1910. (Coleção Rui Barbosa, Arquivo Histórico, FCRB)

O COMMERCIO DA RUA DO OUVIDOR

Sandwich man; drawing by Julião Machado, representing "business on rua do Ouvidor." (*A Cigarra*, Sept. 19, 1895)

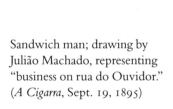

Humorous ad designed by the novelist Aluísio de Azevedo during the period (1876–1878) in which he worked as a caricaturist in the Rio press; published on March 24, 1877, in *O Mequetrefe*.

Advertisement for Lacta chocolates on the back cover of the first issue of the monthly art magazine *Klaxon* (São Paulo, May 15, 1922).

First auto race in São Paulo, from Parque da Antárctica to Itapecerica, an eighty-kilometer circuit, said by *Careta* magazine, in 1908, to be "the first of its kind in South America." The winner was Sílvio Penteado.

Cover by K–Lixto (pen name of Calisto Cordeiro) of *Fon Fon*, a magazine whose name is a representation of the sound of a car horn, a symbol of modernity. (*Fon Fon*, Apr. 16, 1910)

Cover of first issue of *Klaxon* (São Paulo, May 15, 1922): again, the automobile horn as emblem of urban modernization.

A "radiotelephony station" on Corcovado Mountain, Rio de Janeiro. Photo by Augusto Malta, Oct. 2, 1922. (Arquivo Malta, FCRB)

Cover by Julião Machado for *A Notícia Ilustrada*, March 17, 1895, on the "recent advent" of the telephone.

Left: Ad for Underwood typewriters, *Careta*, Mar. 8, 1919.

Below: Ad for Underwood typewriters, *Careta*, June 14, 1919.

CHAPTER 5

Typing Away

Let us return to the typewriter, as in the beginning—or not exactly the typewriter, but printed images of typewriters, extremely detailed images of the various models and makes of typewriters, sometimes featured prominently in the advertisement pages of Brazilian illustrated magazines of the 1910's and 1920's.

For instance, the June 14, 1919, issue of *Careta* contained, in a space of only sixteen pages, two typewriter ads. One of them takes up half a page. Three-quarters of the space of the ad is occupied by a drawing of an "Underwood Standard Typewriter No. 5." The machine is shown in full detail: the keys, the ribbon, the paper carriage, the types, the margin stops, all are visible. The design of the typewriter itself is the ad's most attractive feature. And the copy invites typists to compare the Underwood with any other brand, "a confrontation that is certain to result in full conviction of the superiority of the UNDERWOOD machine." That typewriters were becoming increasingly popular is clear: "Payment may be made in small monthly installments, and we accept used typewriters as part of the payment."

Two pages later, in the same issue, another ad fills the lower half of the page. A thick black circle frames a photograph of a "Royal Typewriter." There is very little text in this advertisement: "Master Model," "Compare the performance," "Write for a catalogue and information," "Casa Edison—Rio, São Paulo, and Bahia." Again, the most seductive argument is the reproduction of the machine, in a central position.

The image of the typewriter, then, grew more and more familiar; the device could be paid for "in small monthly installments" and came in a number of different models, some of them portable.[1] By the mid-1920's, the typewriter had become the archetypal image for the mixture of fascination and fear that the new technical world inspired in the Brazilian writers of the period, at a time when perceptions of technology and the relations between cultural production and modern artifacts were changing fast. In works of the decade, the typewriter was not only depicted differently but also at times seemed to act as a de facto interlocutor in the process of literary creation.

A significant indicator of the changing attitudes in relation to typing is to be found in a letter by Mário de Andrade to Manuel Bandeira, dated April 18, 1925. In it, Mário speaks of his acquisition (on the installment plan) of a typewriter, of his early reactions to its mechanical noise, and of his gradual achievement of a closer intimacy with its mechanisms:

Dearest Manuel, I hereby announce that I have bought this typewriter. If you were here you'd certainly congratulate me for it, just to see how happy I am. On the blessed installment plan, to be sure. Funny thing, so far I feel totally hampered by the fact of writing straight on the machine. My ideas are frightened away by the noise, I myself feel frightened, I've lost touch with my ideas.

That's it: I've lost touch. I can't find them anymore. But I'm sure this will pass, and now you'll be getting really good letters from me. (Andrade 1966a: 97)[2]

Fourteen years after Lima Barreto published his *crônica* "Esta minha letra … ," and seventeen years after Monteiro Lobato first tried to persuade Godofredo Rangel to type his texts, Mário de Andrade's letter suggests that earlier misgivings about typewriters had not yet died away completely. But those misgivings are expressed in a typewritten text. Besides, Mário, unlike Lobato, is not talking about making fair copies: he writes "straight on the machine." And, unlike Lima Barreto, he does not find the idea of duplicating his work "wearisome" or "disgusting"; instead, he is "frightened" by the possibility of losing touch with his ideas. This, however, does not make him take up writing by hand as an exercise in craftsmanship or nostalgia; rather, Mário seems to think of the typewriter as an interlocutor to which he must adjust necessarily: "But I'm sure this will pass," he says, reassuring himself as well as Bandeira. And as he writes, he gradually personalizes the typewriter and grows used to the activity of typing:

And now it's going to be like this: a fifteen-minute break now and then, and I'll be back typing away at my Manuela. Manuela is the name of the typewriter, an homage to you. The idea has just come into my mind. I didn't stop to think or anything: it's Manuela now. So you see, the homage came straight from my heart. (Andrade 1966a: 98)

The typewriter was no longer "disgusting" or frightening but the object of affection. Not only the perception of the typewriter had changed, but also that of a whole landscape of apparatuses, a world of images, and also the literary technique that made it possible to describe the inevitable contacts and confrontations with this world.

In this way the transition was made from a situation in which machines were objects out of their proper place, like the gramophone in *Vida ociosa*, in a literature that affirmed its "calligraphic" character in opposition to industry, to one in which the typewriter began to interfere directly with literary production.

An example is given by Mário de Andrade's poem "Máquina-de-escrever" (Typewriter), from *Losango cáqui*, written around the same time as the letter to Bandeira about the purchase of "Manuela." In this poem, the mediation of the machine, with its standardized type and its fast-paced tapping, is not only the subject of the poem but also what shapes it. This mediation is no longer concealed but shown off; the idea is to make explicit the graphic-poetic process of composition of the text. And, of course, there is no intention of disguising any standardization in "interiors" or in poems that aspire to the condition of pure artifacts, landscapes of a unique self.

"Máquina-de-escrever" begins with an exhibition of mechanical types and industrial brand names:

> BDGZ, Remington.
> For all the letters we write.
> Mechanical echo
> Of fleeting feelings typed into words.
> Haste, much haste.
>> Once someone stole my brother's typewriter
>> This must go into verse too
>> Because he couldn't afford to buy a new one.
> Mechanical equality,
> Love hate sadness …
> And the ironical smiles
> For all the letters we write …
> Evil-doers and Presidents
> Writing with the same letters …
>> Equality
>> Liberty
>> Fraternity, period.
> Unification of all hands …
>
> (Andrade 1966b: 70–71)

"Unification of all hands," "the same letters," "mechanical equality"—standardization seems to smile ironically at tyrannical subjectivity and one of its major forms of expression: letter writing. "And the ironical smiles / For all the letters we write," meaning all kinds of motivation for letters written to all kinds of addressees: letters of courtesy, business letters, love letters. Standardized type is used to produce texts that are suddenly seen to be as standardized as mass-produced goods:

> All loves beginning
> With L's that look just alike …
> The unfaithful husband,
> The unfaithful wife,
> Lovers children boyfriends and girlfriends …

Letters, feelings, loves—they all "look just alike" when written with standardized type. And Mário de Andrade does more than mock passionate love letters; he also questions some of the most aura-charged recesses of literature with this succession of "mechanical echoes." The poem turns into a letter of condolences, or a request for money, always following the formulas of letter-writing manuals. All that is left of the lyrical subject is "the handwritten signature." Writing is reduced to a discontinuous activity, marked by the mechanical tapping of keys; the interruptions have a double function: sometimes they are an ironic context for tears and emotion, sometimes a critical interval between writing and confession. Thus the poem discusses, in its final stanzas, the impossibility of the subject's expressing his or her ecstasy, always interrupted by mechanical errors, the typewriter's lies:

> Tap … Oops!
> There goes the letter O.
> No more astonishments
> For souls amazed before life!
> All anxieties disturbed!
> I can no longer express my ecstasy
> Before your flame-red hair!
>
> The exclamation point in the interjection came out
>   in the wrong place!
> My emotion
> Forgot to backspace.
> So a line was left
> Just like a falling teardrop
> With a final stop next to it.

But I cried no tears, I just went "Oh!"
Before your flame-red hair.
The typewriter lied!
You know how cheerful I am
And how I like to kiss your morning eyes.
See you next Wednesday, the 11th.

I type two lower-case L's.
And then I sign by hand.

Even as he mentions the impossibility of communicating his own emotions, this poetic subject converted into a handwritten signature seems to say to the reader that any attempt to read the typed characters and punctuation signs according to an "expressive" system of analogies is bound to fail. And if the exclamation point comes out looking like a teardrop followed by a period, perhaps the apparent teardrop is really no more than a typo. What Mário de Andrade seems to be suggesting in "Máquina-de-escrever" is that a new dimension should be incorporated into literary reception; that texts should be examined in their graphic materiality, as a set of letters and signs typed or printed on paper.

Just as the awareness of these technical mediations began to shape literary production—first through literal mimesis, displacement, or stylization, as had occurred since the 1890's and by the 1920's had been achieved through the systematic use of methods and materials borrowed from the world of technology—the ways of reading literary texts were also invited to change, to give up timeworn solutions that had become automatic. It is understandable, then, that the best fiction works of the 1920's—Oswald de Andrade's *Memórias sentimentais de João Miramar* and *Serafim Ponte Grande*, Mário de Andrade's *Macunaíma*, and António de Alcântara Machado's *Pathé Baby*—did not really set the pattern for later Brazilian fiction. Of the poetry of the period, what was mostly imitated, to the point of dilution, was the colloquial tone, with its humorous clichés, and not its ironic attack on pure artifact, on tyrannical subjectivity, and—most important— on a literature that sacralizes its own place and those of its producer and its reader. This sacralization was undertaken either by the faithful rendering of private selves and a national character or by desperate attempts to reconstruct the corpses that the literature of the 1920's exhibited in public even as it winked at its equally ruthless accomplice in these murders: technology. However, the critical texts of Oswald de Andrade, for instance, combine this complicity with censure; as "antimechanisms," his writings do not submit to the tyrannies of intimacy, to the portrayal of the national character, or to servile imitation of the technical landscape. What they aspire to is appropriation, a form of serial murder.

This was a difficult problem even for constantly changing restorers, who were quite capable of donning the garb of memorialists, neo-naturalists, or spiritualists: "After the first death, there is no other," as Dylan Thomas put it.[3] That is why much of post-1920's literary production seems to be engaged in a project of systematic concealment of this death. After the first death, there are a series of attempts at resurrection—no, not resurrection, but concealment of the corpses, so as to pretend that no death had occurred, to make the deaths invisible, to conceal the many death certificates that are subtly diffused throughout the fiction and poetry of the 1920's. The proliferation of such murders was one of the specialties of the literature of this period; and the inevitable sound track for these deaths was the mechanical clicking of presses and cameras and typewriters.

Reference Matter

Notes

Chapter 1

1. See Paes 1985: 72–74. In this essay, after stating that "emphasis on ornamentation" was "the most conspicuous feature of art nouveau," Paes establishes a distinction between surface and consubstantial ornamentation. Surface ornamentation accounts for much of the urban fiction of the period (João do Rio, Afrânio Peixoto, Théo Filho, Benjamin Costallat, and Toledo Malta), in addition to "façade regionalism" (which includes the work of Alcides Maia, Afonso Arinos, Valdomiro Silveira, and Hugo de Carvalho Ramos). Its hallmarks, according to Paes, are "surface costumbrismo" and "showy verbalism," ornaments intended to "disguise the poverty of the fictional material." As examples of consubstantiality between ornament and narrative, Paes mentions Simões Lopes Neto and Euclides da Cunha.

2. Clearly, however, Hardman's primary interest is not to reexamine premodernism but to study the birth of the Brazilian working class and its culture during this period. But at this point in his book the author examines traditional conceptions of premodernist literature.

3. The *crônica* is a journalistic form of some importance in Brazilian literature, typically less serious than the essay, focusing on contemporary life and sometimes bordering on light fiction. *A crônica* (1992) is an anthology of the genre. —Trans.

Chapter 2

1. On Lima Barreto's journalistic work, see Barbosa 1981, especially pp. 278–91, and Sevcenko 1983: 161–98.

2. In this text, Gumbrecht suggests the possibility of associating with a functional history and a history of the media the mental structures associated

with the production and reception of texts, to replace a "history of literary forms only."

3. The phrase is used in Candido 1984.

Chapter 3

1. On this, see Vasquez 1985. See also Scharf 1986: 47.

2. See Araújo 1976. The filming, by Afonso Segreto, took place on June 19 and 29 and July 5.

3. The phrase appears in Merquior 1979: 192.

4. On the birth of commercial advertising in Europe, see Habermas 1978: 189–204.

5. The ad came out in the April 5, 1913, issue of *Fon-Fon* and is reproduced in *Nosso século* 1985, 2: 64.

6. Hallewell 1985: 253. On the pioneering role of Lobato as publisher, see Lobato 1968 and Hallewell 1985. It is also important to keep in mind the fact, underscored by Edgard Cavalheiro, that up to the late 1920's "there had not been a truly Brazilian publisher. Garnier, Briguiet, and others operated out of France. A few publishing houses risked putting out a book now and then; these books were usually badly printed, and their distribution was almost nonexistent" (quoted in Fiorentino 1982: 10). But we should also remember such figures as Francisco de Paula Brito, journalist, typographer, bookseller, and publisher, who played a fundamental role in Brazil during the Romantic period (on this, see Jardim 1965). Nonetheless, it should be stressed that the situation of Brazilian publishers in the early twentieth century was quite difficult. See Gomes 1983: 39: "Up to 1914, books were published by European firms only. There were no specialized publishing companies in Brazil. The printing shops handled all kinds of materials and were not prepared for such a heavy, industrial-scale activity as printing books." Gomes also notes that in all of Brazil there were at the time "no more than about thirty bookstores" (p. 40), and that libraries were created by law but were not minimally equipped to become operational. Access to what few libraries actually existed was quite restricted. "Some libraries opened once a week only, on Sunday afternoons, while others opened daily, from 5 to 9 P.M., or from 10 A.M. to 3 P.M." (p. 54).

7. Quoted in Machado Neto 1973: 215. Machado Neto makes some valuable comments on the tendency of Brazilian men of letters to present themselves as attractions. One of the ways to do this was to form salons and groups and engage in polemics: "It was necessary to fight over the small reading public. This involved group behavior (salons), wars between literary coteries, polemics, mutual praising, martial metaphors, protections and persecutions" (p. 164). Another was to make their everyday lives newsworthy and to ornament their own figures as much as possible: "The eyes of the public were open to the exuberant lives of

writers, thanks to literary journalism, and their lives became a major topic in the literary columns of newspapers" (p. 221).

8. José Agudo's real name was José da Costa Sampaio. For more information, see Martins 1977–78, 5: 512–13, 532–37.

9. On the early history of motion pictures in São Paulo, see Galvão 1975.

10. Penumbrismo was a literary tendency from "the transition period between the end of symbolism and early modernism," according to Octávio Filho (1970: 67). It was characterized by "marked poetical *intimism*" (p. 67), by the emphasis on shadows, silence, mystery, and dusky tones; among its best-known practitioners were Mário Pederneiras, Ribeiro Couto, Gonzaga Duque, Lima Campos, Álvaro Moreira, Felippe d'Oliveira, Eduardo Guimaraens, Homero Prates, and Guilherme de Almeida. The term "penumbrista" comes from the title of an article by Ronald de Carvalho—"Poesia da penumbra" (The poetry of penumbra)—on Ribeiro Couto's *O jardim das confidências*. See also Goldstein 1983.

11. This information is given by Raul Pederneiras, quoted in Lima 1969, 1: 137.

12. See Needell 1987. Detailed information and slightly different figures on literacy are given by Gomes: "As to the literacy rate, it was 14 percent in 1890, rising to 25.5 percent by 1900. This suggests that the literacy policies of the first decades of republican government had some effect. But in the following two decades there was no growth at all: the literacy rate in 1920 was still 25.5 percent" (Gomes 1983: 33).

13. For Bilac's humorous verse and rhymed *crônicas*, see the chapters "Musa alegre" and "A conquista da tranqüilidade" of Pontes 1944, and Magalhães 1974: 202–25.

14. The phrase is from Adorno and Horkheimer 1985: 121.

15. A detailed account is given in Meneses 1966: 359–62.

16. On Oswald de Andrade's prose, see also two essays by Haroldo de Campos, "Miramar na mira" and "Serafim: Um grande não-livro," both included in Andrade 1975.

17. On Juó Bannanére (pen name of Alexandre Ribeiro Marcondes Machado), see Carelli 1985: 103–22.

Chapter 4

1. On the use of *raisonneurs* in the early-twentieth-century proletarian theater of São Paulo, see Vargas and Lima 1980.

2. See Taborda et al. 1986: 22: "Ornament, abandoned by later modern architecture, was abundant in the eclectic style. It may also be seen in the letterings that appear in friezes of buildings influenced by classical models; the dates proclaim the pride in belonging to a modern period, and the monograms of the proprietors are imposing."

3. On Lopes Neto, see "Simões Lopes Neto" and "A salamanca do jarau," two essays included in Meyer 1986: 551–82, and "A ficção desmascarada," the next-to-last chapter of Leite 1978.

4. Here it might be worthwhile to transcribe Euclides da Cunha's description of the photographing of Antônio Conselheiro's body, near the end of *Rebellion in the Backlands*:

"The settlement fell on the fifth. On the sixth they completed the work of destroying and dismantling the houses—5,200 of them by careful count.

"Previously, at dawn that day, a commission assigned to the task had discovered the corpse of Antônio Conselheiro. It was lying in one of the huts next to the arbor. After a shallow layer of earth had been removed, the body appeared wrapped in a sorry shroud—a filthy sheet—over which pious hands had strewn a few withered flowers. There, resting upon a reed mat, were the last remains of the 'notorious and barbarous agitator.' They were in a fetid condition. Clothed in his old blue canvas tunic, his face swollen and hideous, the deep-sunken eyes filled with dirt, the Counselor would not have been recognizable to those who in the course of his life had known him most intimately.

"They carefully disinterred the body, precious relic that it was—the sole prize, the only spoils of war this conflict had to offer!—taking the greatest of precautions to see that it did not fall apart, in which case they would have had nothing but a disgusting mass of rotting tissues in their hands. They photographed it afterward and drew up an affidavit in due form, certifying its identity; for the entire nation must be terribly convinced that at last this terrible foe had been done away with." (Cunha 1944: 475–6.)

5. And not just caricaturists: often the covers of novels or volumes of *crônicas* or poetry suggested the idea of surface-only characters, of mere structures of lines and planes. One example of an art nouveau cover in which perspective is almost eliminated is Cornélio Pena's design for Silvino Olavo's *Sombra iluminada* (1927): it shows a somewhat sinister figure, with emaciated hands covered with rings and bracelets, the head covered by a purple cape; it is echoed by a yellow shape, as flat as the figure itself, against a purple background with yellow vertical stripes. An ironic example of the visual exploration of depthless characters and texts is the cover of Costallat's *Mutt, Jeff & Cia.* (1922), designed by the author himself. The draftsmanship is visibly amateurish, with ink blots, apparently a protest against the clean look, the arabesques, and the clear lines that characterize most book covers of the period. Instead of mythological figures like those in Cornélio Pena's cover for João Ribeiro Pinheiro's *Dança de Pan* (1925), or an art nouveau woman's profile as in Correia Dias's cover for *Nós* (1917), or the pastiche of old illuminations made by Paim for the cover of Menotti del Picchia's *As máscaras* (1919), the cover of *Mutt, Jeff & Cia.* shows two larger figures, one done in circles and curves, the other in rectangles and straight lines, together with a number of smaller figures, all quite amateurish-looking. This ironic design seems to prefigure some

of the best covers of the 1920's, such as Paim's for Alcântara Machado's *Pathé Baby*, Tarsila do Amaral's for Oswald de Andrade's *Pau-Brasil*, and Oswald's own design for "Primeiro caderno de poesia do aluno de poesia Oswald de Andrade."

6. Brás Cubas is the protagonist of *Memórias Póstumas de Brás Cubas*, a novel originally published by Machado de Assis from March 15 to December 15, 1880, in *Revista Brasiliera*, and in book form the following year. Conselheiro Aires—a character in and the supposed author of *Esaú e Jacó* (1904), as is explained in an opening section written in the third person—is also the narrator of *Memorial de Aires* (1908), Machado de Assis's last novel. Quincas Borba—a character whose "humanism" is a gloss not only on nineteenth-century evolutionism but also on the narrative discourse of *Memórias Póstumas de Brás Cubas*—reappears in *Quincas Borba* (Philosopher or dog; originally published in installments in the "illustrated newspaper" *A Estação* and in book form in 1891). But the main character in *Quincas Borba* is Rubião, who, in the fourteenth chapter of the novel, inherits all of Quincas's fortune under the condition that he keep the dead man's beloved dog, also named Quincas Borba.

7. See Paes 1985: 72–73: "The theme of the 'eternal feminine,' which in art nouveau literature appears as the stereotype of the modern woman, freed from bourgeois prejudices—though the price of this freedom may be a sort of genteel prostitution—generated a voluminous love-nest literature, representative of which are the novels of Benjamin Costallat and Hilário Tácito . . . as well as the first two volumes of Oswald de Andrade's *Os condenados* trilogy." Costallat's *Mlle. Cinéma* surely may be read from this viewpoint, but Oswald's novels and *Madame Pommery* invite other possible readings.

8. Goldstein's interpretation of penumbrismo has been of fundamental importance to my analysis of early-twentieth-century Brazilian "poetry of interiors."

9. The phrase "figurations of privacy" is borrowed from Lafetá 1986.

10. For instance, the still lifes of the São Paulo painter Pedro Alexandrino (1864–1942), full of showy details and objects of various kinds, are characterized by mannerism and the desire to create images of pure artifice, like those in Parnassian and neo-Parnassian poetry.

11. Candido uses the phrase "pure artifact" in "No coração do silêncio," an analysis of Alberto de Oliveira's poem "Fantástica." See Candido 1985: 67.

12. "Um prego! Mais outro prego! … " was originally published in Magalhães 1920, but I am quoting from its reprinting in Muricy 1973, 2: 930.

13. The Santa Casa is the institution responsible for managing hospitals and cemeteries.—Trans.

14. This does not mean that before the 1920's there had been no critical appropriation of technology, or that the relations between literature and the technological and industrial landscape in Brazil may be seen in terms of evolutionist linearity. One need only think of Raul Pompéia's attack on the nascent advertising industry in *O Ateneu*, or Kilkerry's *crônicas* in the 1910's, or—outside

the field of literature—Valério Vieira's turn-of-the-century photomontage "Os 30 Valérios," to be reminded that there had been fine, and quite critical, instances of the dialogue with technology long before the 1920's.

15. My attention was drawn to Artur Azevedo's *crônicas* about the cinematograph by Aluísio Azevedo Sobrinho; see Azevedo Sobrinho 1961.

Chapter 5

1. At the Arquivo Museu da Literatura, Fundação Casa de Ruy Barbosa, Plínio Doyle showed me a curious advertisement for a Corona typewriter from the 1910's. The top part of the full-page ad included two photographs: one of Lauro Müller, a member of the Brazilian Academy of Letters and then (1912–1917) minister of foreign affairs; to the right, a photograph of a portable Corona typewriter. The text said: "Mr. Lauro Müller, Minister of Foreign Affairs, on his trip to North America took with him a CORONA, the last word in portable typewriters. . . . For the up-to-date traveler, whether statesman, professional, or businessman, a *Corona* is as useful as an office phone."

2. I am indebted to Homero Senna, who brought to my attention this letter, which has been of great use in the development of my argument.

3. This is the last line of Thomas's "A Refusal to Mourn the Death, by Fire, of a Child in London." See Thomas 1980: 94.

Bibliography

Adorno, Theodor W., and Max Horkheimer. 1985. *Dialética do esclarecimento: Fragmentos filosóficos*. Trans. Guido Antonio de Almeida. Rio de Janeiro: Jorge Zahar.

Agudo, José. 1912. *Gente rica (cenas da vida paulistana)*. São Paulo: Emp. Tip. Ed. O Pensamento.

Almeida, Guilherme. 1929. *Simplicidade (versos escritos entre 1910 e 1916)*. São Paulo: Companhia Editora Nacional.

Almeida, Júlia Lopes de. 1923. *A isca*. Rio de Janeiro: Leite Ribeiro.

Amaral, Aracy. 1970. *Artes plásticas na Semana de 22*. São Paulo: Perspectiva.

Andrade, Mário de. 1966a. *Cartas a Manuel Bandeira*. Rio de Janeiro: Edições de Ouro.

———. 1966b. *Poesias completas*. São Paulo: Martins.

———. 1968. *Hallucinated City*. Trans. Jack E. Tomlins. Kingsport, Tenn.: Vanderbilt University Press.

Andrade, Oswald de. 1974. *Poesias reunidas. Obras completas*. Vol. 7. Rio de Janeiro: Civilização Brasileira.

———. 1975. *Memórias sentimentais de João Miramar e Serafim Ponte Grande. Obras completas*. Vol. 2. Rio de Janeiro: Civilização Brasileira.

Anjos, Augusto dos. 1971. *Eu. outras poesias. Poemas esquecidos*. Ed. Antonio Houaiss. 31st ed. Rio de Janeiro: Livraria São José.

Araújo, Vicente de Paula. 1976. *A Bela Época do cinema brasileiro*. São Paulo: Perspectiva.

Azevedo, Artur, and Sampaio Moreira. 1887. *O carioca*. Rio de Janeiro: Emp. Ed. Diário de Notícias.

Azevedo Sobrinho, Aluísio. 1961. "Arthur Azevedo, o primeiro cronista cinematográfico da cidade." Unsigned article. *Revista de Teatro da SBAT* 320 (March–April).

Barbosa, Francisco de Assis. 1981. *A vida de Lima Barreto (1881–1922)*. Rio de Janeiro: José Olympio / MEC.

Barreto, A. H. Lima. 1956. *Feiras e mafuás*. São Paulo: Brasiliense.

———. 1978. *Recordações do escrivão Isaías Caminha*. São Paulo: Brasiliense.

———. 1985. *Os bruzundangas*. São Paulo: Ática.

———. n.d. *Vida e morte de M. J. Gonzaga de Sá*. Rio de Janeiro: Ediouro.

Baudrillard, Jean. 1975. *A sociedade de consumo*. Lisbon: Edições 70.

Benjamin, Walter. 1978. "The Author as Producer." Trans. Edmund Jephcott. In *Essays, Aphorisms, Autobiographical Writings*. New York: Shocken.

———. 1985. "A obra de arte na era de sua reprodutibilidade ténica" (1st version). Trans. Sérgio Paulo Rouanet. In *Obras escolhidas*. São Paulo: Brasiliense.

Bilac, Olavo. 1919. *Tarde*. Rio de Janeiro: Francisco Alves.

———. 1978. *Poesias*. Rio de Janeiro: Edições de Ouro.

Bosi, Alfredo. 1978. *História geral da civilização brasileira*. Part 3, Vol. 2. Rio de Janeiro: Difel.

———. 1985. *História concisa da literatura brasileira*. 3d ed. São Paulo: Cultrix.

———. n.d. *O Pré-Modernismo*. 5th ed. São Paulo: Cultrix.

Brayner, Sônia. 1979. *Labirinto do espaço romanesco*. Rio de Janeiro/Brasília: Civilização Brasileira/INL.

Brito, Mário da Silva. 1978. *História do Modernismo brasileiro: Antecedentes da Semana de Arte Moderna*. Rio de Janeiro: Civilização Brasileira.

Brito, Ronaldo, et al. 1983. *Sete ensaios sobre o Modernismo*. Rio de Janeiro: Funarte.

Broca, Brito. 1960. *A vida literária no Brasil—1900*. Rio de Janeiro: José Olympio.

Campofiorito, Quirino. 1983. *História da pintura brasileira no século XIX*. 5 vols. Rio de Janeiro: Pinakotheke.

Campos, Augusto de. 1985. *Revisão de Kilkerry*. 2d ed. São Paulo: Brasiliense.

Campos, Haroldo de. 1974. "Uma poética da radicalidade." In Andrade 1974, Vol. 7.

———. 1975. "Miramar na Mira." In Andrade 1975.

———. 1984. "Serafim: Um grande não-livro." In Andrade 1975.

Candido, Antonio. 1976. *Literatura e sociedade*. São Paulo: Nacional.

———. 1980. *Teresina etc*. Rio de Janeiro: Paz e Terra.

———. 1984. "Escrita caligráfica." *Suplemento Literário Minas Gerais* 948 (December 1).

———. 1985. *Na sala de aula: Caderno de análise literária*. São Paulo: Ática.

Candido, Antonio, and J. Aderaldo Castelo. 1981. *Do romantismo ao simbolismo*. São Paulo: Difel.

Carelli, Mário. 1985. *Carcamanos & comendadores. Os italianos de São Paulo: Da realidade à ficção (1919–1930)*. São Paulo: Ática.

Carpeaux, Otto Maria. 1951. *Pequena bibliografia crítica da literatura brasileira*. Rio de Janeiro: MEC.

Carvalho, José Murilo de. 1987. *Os bestializados: O Rio de Janeiro e a República que não foi*. São Paulo: Companhia das Letras.

Chalmers, Vera M. 1976. *3 linhas e 4 verdades—O jornalismo de Oswald de Andrade*. São Paulo: Duas Cidades.

Correa, Raimundo. 1922. *Poesias*. 4th ed. Rio de Janeiro/Lisbon/Oporto: Anuário do Brasil/Seara Nova/Renascença Portuguesa.

Costa Lima, Luiz. 1968. *Lira e antilira*. Rio de Janeiro: Civilização Brasileira.

Costallat, Benjamin. n.d. *Mutt, Jeff & Cia. (Crônicas)*. 2d ed. Rio de Janeiro: Leite Ribeiro.

Coutinho, Afrânio, ed. 1969. *A literatura no Brasil*. Vol. 4. Rio de Janeiro: Sul Americana.

Couto, Ribeiro. 1960. *Poesias reunidas*. Rio de Janeiro: José Olympio.

A Crônica: O gênero, sua fixação e suas transformações no Brasil. 1992. Rio de Janeiro/Campinas: Fundação Casa de Rui Barbosa/Unicamp.

Cunha, Euclides da. 1944. *Rebellion in the Backlands*. Trans. Samuel Putnam. Chicago: University of Chicago Press.

Dimas, Antônio. 1983. *Tempos eufóricos*. São Paulo: Ática.

Estrada, Luiz de Gonzaga Duque. 1910. *Graves & frívolos (por assuntos de Arte)*. Lisbon: Liv. Clássica Ed.

———. 1971. *Mocidade morta*. Rio de Janeiro: INL/MEC.

Ferreira, Paulo Roberto. 1986. "Do kinetoscópio ao ominographo." *Filme cultura* 47.

Ferrez, Gilberto. 1985. *A fotografia no Brasil: 1840–1900*. Rio de Janeiro: Funarte/Pró-Memória.

Fiorentino, Teresinha A. del. 1982. *Prosa de ficção em São Paulo: Produção e consumo (1900–1922)*. São Paulo: Hucitec/Secretaria de Estado da Cultura.

Flusser, Vilém. 1985. *Filosofia da caixa preta*. São Paulo: Hucitec.

Franceschi, Humberto Moraes. 1984. *Registro sonoro por meios mecânicos no Brasil*. Rio de Janeiro: Studio HMF.

Freyre, Gilberto. 1979. *O escravo nos anúncios de jornais brasileiros do século XIX*. São Paulo/Brasília: Nacional/Instituto Joaquim Nabuco de Pesquisas Sociais.

Galvão, Maria Rita Eliezer. 1975. *Crônica do cinema paulistano*. São Paulo: Ática.

Goldstein, Norma. 1983. *Do Penumbrismo ao Modernismo*. São Paulo: Ática.

Gomes, Sônia de Conti. 1983. *Bibliotecas e sociedade na Primeira República*. São Paulo: Pioneira.

Grandville, J. J. 1842. *Scènes de la vie privée et publiçue des animaux*. Vol. 2. Paris: J. Hetzel et Paulin.

Gumbrecht, Hans Ulrich. 1985. "The Body versus the Printing Press: Media in the Early Modern Period, Mentalities in the Reign of Castille, and Another History of Literary Forms." *Poetics* 14, nos. 3/4 (August): 209–27.

Habermas, Jürgen. 1978. *L'Espace publique: Archéologie de la publicité comme dimension constitutive de la société bourgeoise*. Paris: Payot.

Hallewell, Laurence. 1985. *O livro no Brasil (sua história)*. São Paulo: T. A. Queiroz/EDUSP.

Hardmann, Francisco Foot. 1983. *Nem pátria, nem patrão! Vida operária e cultura anarquista no Brasil.* São Paulo: Companhia das Letras.

———. 1988. *Trem fantasma (Espetáculos do maquinismo na transição à modernidade).* São Paulo: Companhia das Letras.

Herkenhoff, Paulo. "Fotografia—O automático e o longo processo de modernização." In Ronaldo Brito et al. 1983. *Sete ensaios sobre o Modernismo.* Rio de Janeiro: Funarte.

Jardim, Eunice Ribeiro. 1965. *Vida e obra de Paula Brito.* Rio de Janeiro: Livraria Brasiliana Editora.

Kandinsky, Wassily. 1994. *Punkt und Linie zu Fläche* (Point and line to plane). In *Complete Writings on Art,* edited by Kenneth C. Lindsay and Peter Vergo. New York: Da Capo Press.

Kossoy, Boris. 1980. *Origens e expansão da fotografia no Brasil—Século XIX.* Rio de Janeiro: Funarte.

Lafetá, João Luiz. 1986. *Figuração da intimidade—Imagens na poesia de Mário de Andrade.* São Paulo: Martins Fontes.

Lajolo, Marisa, and Regina Zilberman. 1984. *Literatura infantil brasileira: História e histórias.* São Paulo: Ática.

Leite, Lígia C. Moraes. 1978. *Regionalismo e Modernismo.* São Paulo: Ática.

Lima, Herman de Castro. 1969. *História da caricatura no Brasil.* 4 vols. Rio de Janeiro: José Olympio.

Lima, Yone Soares de. 1985. *A ilustração na produção literária—São Paulo—Década de vinte.* São Paulo: IEB/USP.

Lobato, Monteiro. 1968. *A barca de Gleyre.* 2 vols. São Paulo: Brasiliense.

Lopes, B. *Poesia.* 1962. Ed. Andrade Muricy. Rio de Janeiro: Agir.

Lopes Neto, J. Simoes. 1957. *Contos gauchescos e lendas do Sul.* Porto Alegre: Globo.

Machado, Antônio de Alcântara. 1983. *Pathé Baby: Obras.* Vol. 2. Rio de Janeiro/Brasília: Civilização Brasileira/INL.

Machado Neto, Antônio Luís. 1973. *Estrutura social da república das letras: Sociologia da vida intelectual brasileira, 1870–1930.* São Paulo: Grijalbo/EDUSP.

Magalhães, Adelino. 1920. *Tumulto da vida.* Rio de Janeiro: Revista dos Tribunais.

Magãlhaes, Raimundo, Jr. 1974. *Olavo Bilac e sua época.* Rio de Janeiro: Americana.

———. 1978. *A vida vertiginosa de João do Rio.* Rio de Janeiro/Brasília: Civilização Brasileira/INL.

Mariano, Olegário. 1911–12. *Evangelho da sombra e do silêncio.* No publisher.

Martins, Luís, ed. 1971. *João do Rio (uma antologia).* Rio de Janeiro: Sabiá/INL.

Martins, Wilson. 1977–78. *História da inteligência brasileira.* Vols. 4, 5, and 6. São Paulo: Cultrix.

Meneses, Emílio de. 1980. *Obra reunida*. Rio de Janeiro/Curitiba: José Olympio/Secretaria da Cultura e do Esporte do Estado do Paraná.

Meneses, Raimundo de. 1949. *Emílio de Meneses—O último boêmio*. 2d ed. São Paulo: Saraiva.

——. 1957. *A vida boêmia de Paula Ney*. São Paulo: Martins.

——. 1966. *Bastos Tigre e "La Belle Époque."* São Paulo: Edart.

Merquior, José Guilherme. 1979. *De Anchieta a Euclides*. Rio de Janeiro: José Olympio.

Meyer, Augusto. 1986. *Textos críticos*. Ed. João Alexandre Barbosa. São Paulo: Perspectiva/INL/Pró-Memória.

Miceli, Sérgio. 1977. *Poder, sexo e letras na República Velha*. São Paulo: Perspectiva.

Miguel Pereira, Lúcia. 1973. *Prosa de ficção (de 1870 a 1920)*. Rio de Janeiro/Brasília: José Olympio/INL.

Moisés, Massaud. 1973. *O Simbolismo*. São Paulo: Cultrix.

Motta, Flávio L. 1983. "Art-nouveau, Modernismo, ecletismo e industrialismo." In *História geral da arte no Brasil*, edited by Walter Zanini. Vol. 1. São Paulo: Instituto Walther Moreira Salles/Fundação Djalma Guimarães.

Motta, Flávio L., et al. 1978. "O Rio da Belle Époque." *Artefato* 5.

Muricy, Andrade. 1973. *Panorama do movimento simbolista brasileiro*. 3 vols. Rio de Janeiro: INL.

Nabuco, Joaquim. 1934. *Minha formação*. São Paulo/Rio de Janeiro: Nacional/Civilização Brasileira.

Needell, Jeffrey D. 1987. *A Tropical Belle Époque: Elite Culture and Society in Turn-of-the-Century Rio de Janeiro*. Cambridge, Eng.: University of Cambridge Press Syndicate.

Nosso século. 1985. Vol. 1, *1900/1910: A era dos bacharéis*. Vol. 2, *1910/1930: Anos de crise e criação*. São Paulo: Abril Cultural/Círculo do Livro.

Octávio Filho, Rodrigo. 1970. *Simbolismo e Penumbrismo*. Rio de Janeiro: Livraria São José.

Paes, José Paulo. 1985. "O *art-nouveau* na literatura brasileira." In *Gregos & baianos*. São Paulo: Brasiliense.

Pederneiras, Mário. 1958. *Poesia*. Rio de Janeiro: Agir.

Pompéia, Raul. 1976. *O Ateneu*. Rio de Janeiro: Francisco Alves.

Pontes, Eloy. 1944. *A vida exuberante de Olavo Bilac*. 2 vols. Rio de Janeiro: José Olympio.

Prado, Antônio Arnoni. 1976. *Lima Barreto: O crítico e a crise*. Rio de Janeiro: Cátedra.

——. 1983. "Mutilados da Belle Époque." In *Os pobres na literatura brasileira*, edited by Roberto Schwarz. São Paulo: Brasiliense.

——. 1983. *1922: Itinerário de uma falsa vanguarda*.

——, ed. 1986. *Libertários no Brasil*. São Paulo: Brasiliense.

Prado, Antônio Arnoni, and Francisco Foot Hardman, eds. 1985. *Contos anarquistas*. São Paulo: Brasiliense.

Rama, Angel. 1985. *A cidade das letras*. São Paulo: Brasiliense.

Ramos, Ricardo. 1985. *Do reclame à comunicação (Pequena história da propaganda no Brasil)*. São Paulo: Atual.

Rangel, Godofredo. n.d. *Vida ociosa*. 3d ed. São Paulo: Melhoramentos.

Reis, Zenir Campos. 1977. *Augusto dos Anjos: Vida e obra*. São Paulo: Ática.

Rio, João do. n.d. [1908]. *O momento literário*. Rio de Janeiro: Garnier.

——. 1909. *Cinematógrafo*. Oporto: Chadron.

——. 1910. *A alma encantadora das ruas*. Rio de Janeiro/Paris: Garnier.

——. 1911. *A profissão de Jacques Pedreira*. Rio de Janeiro/Paris: H. Garnier.

——. 1918. *A correspondência de uma estação de cura*. Rio de Janeiro: Leite Ribeiro & Maurillo.

——. n.d. *Eva*. Rio de Janeiro: Villas Boas & C.

Santiago, Silviano. 1982. *Vale quanto pesa*. Rio de Janeiro: Paz e Terra.

——. 1983. "Fechado para balanço." In Silviano Santiago et al., *O livro do seminário*. São Paulo: L. R. Editores.

Scharf, Aaron. 1986. *Art and Photography*. London: Penguin.

Schwartz, Jorge. 1983. *Vanguarda e cosmopolitismo*. São Paulo: Perspectiva.

Schwarz, Roberto. 1981. *A sereia e o desconfiado*. Rio de Janeiro: Paz e Terra.

Schwarz, Roberto, et al. 1982. *Machado de Assis: Antologia & estudos*. São Paulo: Ática.

Sevcenko, Nicolau. 1983. *Literatura como missão: Tensões sociais e criação cultural na Primeira República*. São Paulo: Brasiliense.

Silva, Geraldo Gomes da. 1986. *Arquitetura do ferro no Brasil*. São Paulo: Nobel.

Silveira, Valdomiro. 1962. *Os caboclos*. Rio de Janeiro: Civilização Brasileira.

Sodré, Nelson Werneck. 1983. *História da imprensa no Brasil*. Rio de Janeiro: Civilização Brasileira.

Sontag, Susan. 1977. *On Photography*. New York: Farrar, Straus and Giroux.

Souza, Gilda de Mello e. 1980. *Exercícios de leitura*. São Paulo: Duas Cidades.

Taborda, Felipe, et al. 1986. *A tipografia na arquitetura do Rio de Janeiro*. Rio de Janeiro: Index.

Tácito, Hilário. 1977. *Madame Pommery*. Vol. 6. São Paulo: Biblioteca "Academia Paulista de Letras."

Thomas, Dylan. 1980. *Collected Poems 1934–1952*. London: Everyman.

Tinhorão, José Ramos. 1981. *Música popular: Do gramofone ao rádio e TV*. São Paulo: Ática.

Vargas, Maria Thereza, and Mariângela Alves de Lima. 1980. *Teatro operário na cidade de São Paulo*. São Paulo: IDART.

Vasconcelos, Ary. 1977. *Panorama de música popular brasileira na "Belle Époque."* Rio de Janeiro: Sant'Anna.

Vasquez, Pedro. 1985. *Dom Pedro II e a fotografia no Brasil*. Rio de Janeiro: Index.

Vaz, Léo. 1920. *O professor Jeremias*. São Paulo: Edição da "Revista do Brasil."

Vieira, João Luiz, and Margareth C. S. Pereira. 1986. "Cinemas cariocas: da Ouvidor à Cinelândia." *Filme cultura* 47.

Wisnik, José Miguel. 1983. *O coro dos contrários: A música em torno da Semana de 22*. São Paulo: Duas Cidades.

Xavier, Ismail. 1978. *Sétima arte: Um culto moderno*. São Paulo: Perspectiva.

Zilio, Carlos. 1982. *A querela do Brasil*. Rio de Janeiro: Funarte.

Index

In this index an "f" after a number indicates a separate reference on the next page, and an "ff" indicates separate references on the next two pages. A continuous discussion over two or more pages is indicated by a span of page numbers, e.g., "57–59." *Passim* is used for a cluster of references in close but not consecutive sequence.

Library of Congress Cataloging-in-Publication Data

Süssekind, Flora.
  [Cinematógrafo de letras. English]
  Cinematograph of words : literature, technique, and modernization
in Brazil / Flora Süssekind ; translated by Paulo Henriques Britto.
    p.   cm. — (Writing science)
  Includes bibliographical references and index.
  ISBN 0-8047-2913-1 (cl.)
  ISBN 0-8047-3063-6 (pbk.)
  1. Brazilian literature—20th century—History and criticism.
2. Literature and technology—Brazil.   3. Technology in literature.
I. Britto, Paulo Henriques. II. Title. III. Series.
PQ9555.S8613   1997
869'.09981—dc21   96-52436
                                                   CIP

⊗ This book is printed on acid-free, recycled paper.

Original printing 1997
Last figure below indicates year of this printing:
06 05 04 03 02 01 00 99 98 97